T747

Higher Techniques to Inner Perfection

Bryce Bond

INNER LIGHT PUBLICATIONS

Editorial Director:
Timothy Green Beckley
Manuscript Production:
Cross-Country Consultants

Cover designed by Barbara Lynn

For foreign and reprint rights, contact:
Inner Light Publications
P.O. Box 753, New Brunswick, N.J. 08903

Contents

Bryce Bond is a top motivation speaker in demand at major universities, corporations, and numerous global organizations. Presently he produces and hosts a TV show, *Dimensions*, dealing with parapsychology, and has recorded six record albums, been disk jockey on a popular New York City radio station, and is author of *A Touch of Alchemy* and *Self Healing: A Personal Transformation*.

Acknowledgments

To GOD for manifesting my creation on this planet, to gain the experiences, to learn the lessons, to create and to eventually manifest his perfection within and without, so I might be able humbly to reflect his divine awareness.

To my friends on both realms, I give THANKS for your support, and those very special beings who worked so closely believing that these thoughts had to materialize, that others might gain a new access route to their own personal enlightenment.

To a very special brother, FRANK DON, who had the courage of his convictions to collaborate with his wisdom and sharing, on this project.

To you all, my LOVE, and heart-felt THANKS.

Preface

There is no place where mind cannot travel, penetrating a curved universe into a spheroid of shaped mind desire. Mind desire gives birth to physical manifestation in matter. Matter forms in the shape of evolutionary mind of spirit desire constantly gestating in cyclic time. Time and space are frozen in form by non-energized mind desire of the one mind expression of exploding compression.

Mind desire manifests mind power which creates energy compression to manifest shaped matter. It holds itself into a freeze frame of mind to awaken mind desire into pulsations of electrical rings of mind, creating patterns between the freeze frames of mind desire! We form our thoughts by the ever changing thought patterns of electrical energies created by Mind Desire.

We are the reflection and expressions of our thoughts—created thought forms made manifest in physical bodies. Whatever we think, we become. Our physical bodies begin to be programmed by our thinking process, and we will portray that reflection until a new thought structure begins. And when a new thought pattern begins, it expands consciousness. It builds a superstructure to awareness.

For all ideas, thoughts, and the expression of emotion are building blocks toward self-revelation, awakening, and lifting the shutters of the mind, the storehouse of all thought and past life experiences. We merely repeat the cycles unconsciously as a mirror looking back at itself. We are in all reality mirrors to each other. Most individuals do not like what they see in themselves—

by the mirror reflected by others.

If we mirror the highest of all life forms (GOD), we would see only perfection in ourselves and in others.

We would be *free* of judgments, for how can we see darkness when we stand in the light?

The darkness dwells in our inability to forgive ourselves for our judgments, our hates, our angers.

The CHOSEN ones are CHOSEN in their own judgement!

Turn on your light by allowing it to be seen by others. Today is your last day on earth. Tomorrow is the re-birth. Let re-birth be FREE, PURE and TRUTHFUL. If others live through spiritual *lack* and *limitations*, allow them their choice. REMEMBER, you cannot share your pearls before time!

One day in the future they will make a great decision to change. Change is constant, and must not be stopped or harnessed. It is a cyclic pulsation of the continuum and expression of consciousness of all creation, a creation that has never stopped, a creation that has always been. Man represents the small specks of imperfection that resists change, to the point of static inertia.

Allow your mind to permeate the atmosphere of your soul; allow it to open to receive the gift of creation that is in continual flow. Keep the mind moving forward, seeking change, manifesting and expressing true perfection within the continuity of life.

Any impression that takes form in the mind and becomes deeply seated will take physical form and manifest itself accordingly. Again, whatever we think we become. We can hold back diluted ideas with procrastination, because they were not desires or honest beliefs, they were only random thoughts swirling about going nowhere, caught in the kaleidoscope of energies within the life-streams which envelop our planet.

We must be able to become focused with our thoughts, and not allow random thoughts to intrude upon our centering and focused consciousness. If they are true desire fixations where intent is clean and clear, then you do give life to the thought forms that we all create.

In turn, these will put us in harmony with the collective

vibrations which manifest themselves in the others. These electrical energies (THOUGHT FORMS) create patterns, from these patterns come desire, will, and the substance that brings all these collected energies into the accomplished desire form.

More and more individuals can see the light, and hear the approach of those spiritual beings, they can read the sign of the times, and there is a sincere desire to help their fellow men, their brothers and sisters. They have reached turning points in their lives and now are reaching in the direction of GOD.

You see the manifestation of the final act in the drama of life expressed on this beautiful EARTH MOTHER—now made sick and diseased and tilting on its axis, like yesterday's hangover. She is in her final hour. Can she in one last fleeting effort stave off the inevitable transformation of this planet?

If all men and women collectively could stand side by side balanced in harmony and love, equally, we could correct our world over night. WE COULD! Women are the polarity that will make it all work, the blending of the two. Man must rid himself of his own distorted view of women, for he keeps peace from happening. When will man grow up? When will he realize that women are equal in every way, the opposites of men? Yet two equally polarized electrical energies manifested in the image of the FATHER—MOTHER merged as the one GOD of all that is. GOD remains the same, only man changes in a constant cycle through the evolutionary spiral of eternity. If you stay in the past, you lose the future!

When we completely surrender to the highest concepts within ourselves, with unquestionable FAITH, miracles begin to happen. But what is a miracle? A miracle is a mode of understanding that when you break through fear, you find love. When you break through darkness, you find light. Each negative provides a positive. Within torment there is peace! As night gives way for the day, you can see again. Everything is attracted to the light.

The light of GOD is so bright that many squint their eyes and DIM the reality of their vision, and their souls.

You lock a man in TOTAL darkness for a year and he will die. Lock man's consciousness in darkness and that too fades into oblivion. We must now more than ever before open our consciousness, and risk the fear of the unknown — to the beauty, to the LOVE, joy and peace that is our birthright. The gifts are always waiting for you. Pick your time (LIFETIME—PAST—FUTURE—PRESENT) and give yourself a preview. You will never look back. You will first discover your own beauty, your own wisdom, you own true peace.

You will come to realize there is only one path, and one road, and it leads back home to the loving FATHER. At that glorious moment in time, you will be ALL light. Never again will you ever walk in darkness....

Bryce Bond interviews chief Druid, Dr. Thomas Maugham, D.Sc. who has been a great inspiration in the author's knowledge of metaphysics.

Self Discovery

Why are we here? What is the purpose of life? Some people say we are here only to eat, drink and be merry, for tomorrow....

Ah, tomorrow. Waiting like a phantom in the wings, tomorrow for this type of person seems fraught with radical, devastating change on their inexorable march to the final step: death.

Do you believe that?

Other people say that life is to be lived to the fullest. And I agree. But to get while the getting is good? That's what many people believe. For we have been taught, as one television commercial paraphrases it, that we only go round once in life, so we better grab for all the gusto we can get. This type of person believes living life to the fullest is like some kind of monopoly game where we try to acquire all things material, then store and hoard our "goodies".

What do you think?

I happen to believe that you—the reader, with this book in hand—has a clue to something beyond these perspectives in life. I believe there is something awakening in you, a quickening taking place that demands an answer to the nagging question: Why am I here?

Maybe you have been successful in the material world. Maybe you have realized your wildest dreams, but in your success have found the experience not a sweet taste but rather a taste like bitter ashes. Consequently, you may have turned from your habitual ways, and in the quiet of the small voice within, asked yourself: Is that all there is?

Or maybe you have toiled the fields, always trying to be the good samaritan, helping others along the way.

But for all your efforts, for all your good intentions, you feel a certain sadness that your efforts have gone unrewarded, whether the reward be that of commendation, praise and approval from others, or the reward of increased self-esteem. Stymied by the lack of apparent reward, perhaps you have asked yourself the question: why?

And like Job beseeching the heavens for the answer to life's apparent inequities, you have demanded some logic or rationale to your own life's work and efforts.

Do you know people who feel overwhelmed by life's complications? People who feel their life has been a series of tragedies? And, when compared to the lot of others, their share of pain and hurt seems so unfair to them. These type of people are likely to say that they feel old and tired, and they have been through enough.

Whatever the reason for asking the question, the questioning of life's purpose begins the first step on the journey along the path.

What path? you might ask.

The path of evolution — the beginning of your journey toward growth and development through living. All the experiences we go through, that continually changing montage of life's incidents and events—they all have one purpose. And that purpose is to hone us and refine us in our evolving as a human being. By coping with personal trials and tribulations, your experiences bring you closer to GOD and closer to the consciousness of realizing yourself as the child of GOD.

So when you become stymied by life and you stop to ask yourself the purpose of your life, do not despair. For you have started your journey, a quest in search of the answer.

When you have become aware of the personal conflicts in your own life, as you start to wonder about the choices you have made, you awaken to surging thoughts that reflect upon the purpose of life. You start to question life—your life. And the questions flood your mind.

Questions such as: Why am I here? What is my purpose on this planet? Why do certain things happen to me, and not to other people?.... What am I supposed to learn?.... Is this all there is?.... Why is life so painful?.... Why must so many suffer?.... Why can't I make a go of it?

These are just a few of the countless questions raised in the minds of those who are unaware.

Although the rampage of unanswered questions may throw you into despondency or total confusion, it is an important time. Remember, confusion is the starting point of wisdom. For what is a question? It is not a quest, a search for understanding?

With all thy getting.... This quest, with its nagging questions, is often triggered by some negative event. The incident may be traumatic, even life-threatening. Or it may come quietly to you, like a subtle feeling within you that something is wrong. Whether traumatic or subtle, these challenges are to be appreciated. They are truly blessings in the disguise of pain.

Some people may ignore these blessings by saying they have learned to live with their pain. They are making excuses. They are looking the other way. They do not want to change. But why?

Because these of people find change too hard to express. Change to them is an unsure journey, of forsaking the known for the unknown. And what if the unknown is worse than the known? Instead, they put off until tomorrow what they could be starting today.

And when tomorrow comes, they will find other reasons not to change. Perhaps they will justify their actions with "I only live one day at a time."

Such rationale depicts the person who is totally unconscious, who has no conception what time of day it is, unaware of who he is or where he or she is. This person thinks life is just one long procession through painful hardships, unpleasant experiences and often he or she believes he or she is the only one suffering.

Even this person will change. Eventually, the pain and torment of their condition will force a change. A change either instigated by themselves or forced upon them by the outside world.

12

Painful experiences provide catalysts in your evolution. They dictate a change. And then the quest begins. Do not worry if you feel at times as though you do not know what to change. Do not be worried if the road toward change seems overwhelming and poorly marked.

The catalyst is the seed of dissatisfaction. Some little thought may be tiny in the beginning, has entered your mind, and your consciousness has started to respond. You are no longer satisfied with your life as you have lived it, and you want something more.

But what? Is it a new car? A new house? A new job? A lover? If you believe it is any of these, then, as you follow your urging, you will find you have started a circuitous course that leads you back to the same general sense of dissatisfaction.

The real quest is not a transition from one material goal to another. It is a search for peace of mind, for enlightenment, and wisdom.

But how do we get there? We get there by walking the road, by living our life.

Through all the joys, all the sorrows, we look beyond the ephemeral to the real. There are many guideposts along the way, any number of markers leading us in the right direction.

Each person's path is different. Each person has his or her own unique set of experiences to go through. These experiences are the lessons of life by which we learn about ourselves, about our true purpose in life, about the errors of our ways in the past so we may correct them in the present.

If you look for the answer in the ways of other people or functions, then you are likely to get on the wrong track. Why? Because every person's lesson in life is different. Life is experienced differently even under similar situations. For each of us is a unique entity, with the divine spark indwelling within each of us, waiting to ignite through our own efforts.

There is much illusion to cut through. Hindu philosophy talks about this illusion as the veil of maya. In Western terms, we know it to be the deceit of appearance. What appears to be real or true may only be a mirage, a distortion of true reality.

Why do we buy into such illusion and distortion? Because from our earliest days, through our parental conditioning, later on by the schooling process, we are taught inaccuracies, distortions and falsehoods, all under the guise of truth and reality.

If you feel yourself to be different, enjoy the sense. For you have started to pull away from the mass consciousness, away from the accepted opinions and standards of society. It may seem a lonely space for you. You may rebel against it. You may wonder what's wrong with you, being different when everyone else is so much the same.

They are really not the same for each of us. We are all different. But in our society, in our learning processes, we discover that to be different is to become the target of some perverse pecking order. Our society demands conformity, for conformity breeds acceptance of the ways and mores of social conditioning.

Is conformity effective? Yes, indeed it is, for it has purged the spirit of individuality within the person seeking to change.

We have all experienced it in our own lives. Perhaps it started with our parents; they wondered why we couldn't be more like our brother, our sister, our uncle Eddie or our aunt Bernice. May be we have had the idea drummed into us that what is good for the goose is good for the gander. "Do not make waves, do not be different." And with the brute force of the collective consciousness as our adversary, we battled for our right to be different, to be individual, to be true to ourselves.

But it is a battle, and some of us may decide we are not strong enough, that it is not worth it, that it is like banging our head against the wall until we finally stop and give up, and give in. If we do that, we may condemn ourselves to a life that may be socially acceptable but not fulfilling. We have to remember that misery loves company.

Self

Today, the way you live, what you do, the manner of inter-acting with others, creates the patterns of your tomorrow. For it is a law of the universe (studies in our material world as the law of physics) that whatever is set into motion must work itself out. In biblical terms we know it in the parable "as ye sow so, too, shall ye reap."

It is in karma that our tomorrows are built upon what we do today.

If you lie, cheat and steal today, perhaps you will get away with it. Momentarily. But over the longer haul, tomorrow or the day after, your choices in action will come back to haunt you.

Take advantage of someone else today, and you will get your turn at being taken advantage of tomorrow.

In the manner of JESUS the CHRIST, we are told to "forgive them for they know not what they do." Unconsciousness, the lack of awareness, may be an excuse for wrong action. But it is truly only that: an excuse. People who seek such excuses feed upon the phrase that ignorance is bliss. But ignorance is not bliss. It is only ignorant.

As individuals, living in the collective stream of conscious-ness, we are growing toward awareness. We are expanding our consciousness and eventually will gain understanding. When? When we use the pain and hardship of our life experiences as the catalysts to our growth; for correcting our inappropriate behavior, for remedying our past ways of action.

Will we take advantage of such golden opportunities? Or will we, instead, decry the slings and arrows of outrageous fortune? Will we, in that supposedly blissful state of ignorance accept the belief that we are the only one suffering? As if we were personally picked by GOD to bear the brunt of life's misfortunes, while others were out having a good time, enjoying themselves and acquiring and hoarding material goods.

If we fail to take advantage of the labor pains in the process of our own re-birthing, then realize that those guides along the way may look at us in a detached manner and utter the word of the one who proved to mankind the victory of spirit over matter. "Forgive them, LORD, for they know not what they do."

To believe that GOD has personally picked us out to experience the scourges of the world is highly egotistical, and is in truth an inaccurate attitude. It is a martyr role, and one that deserves all the misfortunes it programs for the person. If you buy into this attitude, then you are likely to feel completely thwarted.

And indeed, you will be. For such an attitude forces you to build up some very heavy limitations. Limitations that are self-imposed and instigate a sense of blaming the world for all of your hardships.

If ever there was a cop out, that's the one. And it is an excuse used by those who are too lazy, who do not want to grow or work through this lifetime. Instead, they make excuses for why they can't take hold of their own lives. With a lack of self worth, and low self esteem, these people cannot love themselves. Nor can they truly love life. Instead, they blame everyone. They blame their parents for being bad parents, for not raising them right, for pigeonholing them into some specific role for which they feel unsuited.

And the one who is likely to get the greatest share of the blame is the one who can give us the most: GOD. But these people lash out, blaming anyone and everyone, except the true culprit: themselves.

It is only when we own up to our responsibility for our evolution, for *UL1*our*UL0* progress through life, that we address our readiness to evolve in this life experience. It takes time. It takes time to grow into awareness. As it takes time for a mighty oak to grow from an acorn, so too, do we need the time to progress in our consciousness, expand our awareness.

Perhaps we do not see the time factor as necessary? With societal conditioning and present attitudes, where we have instant breakfast, instant coffee, instant gratification and instant enlightenment, we lose sight of the true process of reality. At this stage in human evolution, one outlet for this instant phenomena craze is the fundamentalist Christian attitude of the "born again. "This attitude allows a belief that we can expiate all our past sins, all our wrong actions, with one quick conversion process.

Being "born again!" While we should not deny the possibility of such a conversion, one profound example is the experience of Saul of Tarsus on the road to Damascus, when he experienced the CHRIST and by this revelation, had a conversion to be the true apostle, Paul. In our day, while such conversion remains a definite possibility, the experience has been misapplied by those "false prophets" who proclaim against the universal law: The real truth of harvesting what you have sown from your past actions.

Time is an essential component in our growth process. You would not expect a child in kindergarten to master university studies. Within the child is the seed which may well grow into the young man or woman ready to engage a university education. The same is true for ourselves and our level of consciousness. We cannot expect someone who has not evolved to the moral action to be moral and upright in their dealings. It is beyond them. So too in our development of consciousness.

Our growth, our development, takes time. For time provides us with the opportunity of experience. True growth comes from experience. It cannot be learned merely by the abstraction contained in some book of knowledge. It must be used; applied. It must come through our errors, our backsliding habits, our realizations of the consequences of past actions we have previously employed.

In our life experience it is important to appreciate where we are right now. Why? Mainly, it gives us the awareness of our self as we truly are. We look at ourselves in the clarity of our present life conditions, without the distortions of ego games—the manipulations of our very being through our wants, needs, and desires, many of which are expected to shore up our sense of insecurity, our lack. Then too, by truly looking at where we are in life, we appreciate the process, the various levels we go through as we advance in life, both through time and in the expansion of our consciousness.

Let me give you an example. Have you ever planted a seed in a paper cup and watched the process as the seed takes to the soil, gestates, germinates, then pops its tiny sprout through the soil to grow in the sunlight, branching out, reaching higher toward that light? At each step of the way, if we are like children sensitive to the wonder, there is pure delight.

In our lives, we continually rid ourselves of the many dragons which live within us. These dragons are the wrong attitudes and wrong actions that we have adapted. The slaying of these dragons is the facing, and owning up to the results of our human emotional ego, the collected clutter of our personality state.

Today is your first step into your tomorrow. Today is the day you can make a firm commitment to free yourself. Free yourself from what? From all the limitations, all those dragons that clutter your path and block your way. If you will make that commitment, you have already begun the process of cleaning out. It is almost like reprogramming yourself, cutting the cord of a habitual response pattern. So when the negative force comes back knocking on your door—no matter what form it may take—you do not have to react the way you have done in the past. Instead, like a warrior ready to slay your own hangups and blockages, you can forcefully shout out: SORRY, THE DRAGON DOES NOT LIVE HERE ANYMORE!

What a glorious experience! What a cause for celebration! Untangling some of the lines of the constrictive webs we have woven for ourselves. Like Gulliver, freeing ourselves from the lilliputians that would keep us restricted, keep us in an attitude of lack, the behavior of fear.

Like the phoenix, that mythical bird of resurrection, burning upon the pyre all our outdated and dying forms and beliefs, freeing ourselves from our own past limitations, opening up to a rebirth within ourselves, to soar even higher. If you are anchored to the ground by weighty burdens, how can you imagine to fly?

The journey within is the pathway to self-discovery. It is lived in the context of time-space, in this lifetime, in the lifetimes of eternity—the lives we have lived, the lives we have to live. Along the way are many pitfalls, traps, temptations, seductions and manipulations of ego personality, the unawakened consciousness, or more literally, the unconscious. To avoid the detours along the path, it is wise to stay in the middle of the road. In so doing, you choose moderation.

And have we not learned the truth in the adage: moderation in all things. For if we have not yet realized that truth, we shall have to learn it in the future. After our immoderation and excesses demand their toll.

Imagine if you will, those of you who drink alcohol and have occasionally tied one on, the hangover of the day after a partying binge. You pay the price. As with everything in life, there is no free lunch. Consequences follow actions, and there is no avoiding it.

How about the times, the feasts of national holidays, when the focus of our bountiful blessings is symbolized in the gargantuan displays of food? Who hasn't gorged himself with incredible amounts of food? Eating well past a sense of fullness, to a point of exhaustion and bloating. And the consequence? Indigestion.

We accept a belief that having a good time means running at our limits because we have been conditioned to do so. But sometimes we forget to link up the price we have paid for our actions. The two examples above are obvious and I am sure you can imagine your own consequences from the above actions.

But what about subtle immoderation? Those excesses that we may not see as excesses. Those seductions that may seem so right, but in their actions are so wrong—– the dragons in sheep's clothing. Can you think of any? How about the ones where we justify our actions because everyone else in doing it? May be we understand, somewhere, deep within our conscience, that what we are doing is not truly right. But we do it anyway. Because everybody else is doing it and if we don't, then we are just being stupid, and we are creating our own blockages and limitations, and....

WAIT A MINUTE. The justifications are only excuses. Remember: it takes time to grow into awareness. And the seductions do not go away at any point along the trip. Another seduction, one that ebbs and flows, is one of self-righteousness. You probably know the adage: a little knowledge is a dangerous thing. Indeed it is.

Self-righteousness is running rampant today. Everybody who has turned, no matter to what degree, from total material focus seems to go through a period of running for some perverse kind of sainthood. It is like everybody who is finding GOD has the way. And like missionaries in the cause of divine right they spread the word to the uninformed, unenlightened. While sharing their insights and marvelling in life's creations is a wonderful delight, these people want you to know and accept their truth as your own. And they may go to the extreme in trying to impress their beliefs upon you, molding your mind, your self expression, your own individual growth according to their specifications.

And it is a case of immoderation. Dogma and doctrine speak of a rigidity. Rigidity is a blockage of energy, and thus is completely out of step with universal reality. Watch for it. It is coming to your local area, down the street, within your own home. It is a danger.

When people start to get religious, the message, the meaning, whether it be the teachings of organized religion or an occult group, people seem to go on a mission. In a sense, they are spurred on by those who have sponsored them, the practitioners of their truth. And various teachers and groups are mushrooming, spreading the way of finding GOD, of touching base with the divinity within themselves.

Immoderation in the cause of some glorious goal is one of the greatest seductions, for indeed it is the most subtle. Today it is growing stronger, in the increasing influence of what we might term in the broadest sense "religion." Religion is extending its influence into our lives, but not in the sense of moral teachings of life understandings. Rather, religion, the institutions devoid of their kernel of truth, are spreading their tentacles, demanding that we accept their own specific sense of the true way, imposing certain beliefs upon society's accepted standards and how we live our lives. All in the name of morality.

It is a seduction we must learn from, in our own personal lives, and in our communities. Mankind has gone through the excesses of dogma in the past with dire consequences: millions of people consumed, at different times, in different ages, all in the name of righteousness. And at present we see the rising of religious groups, carrying on their holy wars. The fundamentalist Islamic rise in the Khomeini regime in Iran, the invasion of the holy Sikh shrine, the Golden Temple in Amritsars, and the consequent assassination of Prime Minister Indira Gandhi by a Sikh fanatic, the Born-Again Christian movement in the United States with its threatening damnation of those who have not found JESUS CHRIST in the same place they believe they have found him.

Religion and morality are both examples of self-righteousness, of the ego's manipulation in allowing you to believe you have the power, or right, to judge another.

You may think I have emphasized this seduction out of all proportion. Not really. Because it is essential we become clear in our perceptions, in order to see Reality as it truly is and not the way we wish to imagine it. We are working toward a phase when we clearly see (clairvoyantly) what is really going on. When we can clearly perceive the seductions, manipulations and the right action.

The seduction in life will push us to the very brink of self-destruction. It constantly pulls us from the path. In elementary school we were taught that the shortest distance between two points is a straight line. It is. But always from abstractions, in life's reality, where we have cycles in action, the inflowing and outflowing, crests and troughs, life's process is more like a lightning bolt, streaking through the sky, indicating the shift from one polarity to another, as if seeking the middle point.

When you are pulled from the path by some seduction or another, do not worry about reaping your consequences. You will.

You have to. But do not waste a lot of time in damning yourself. Flogging yourself for the errors of your ways is only acting upon your judgement of your ways. It is another seduction.

Life is a constant change. As individuals, we tend to take on the conditions of our environment. We work through those conditions, learning the lessons contained in those experiences, and eventually we move on to another environment, taking on the conditions of that environment, gaining new experiences or different experiences from that environment, eventually learning the lessons of that environment.

Experience is GROWTH. The moment you stop growing, you start to die. You do not have to, though.

Life provides us with a multitude of varied experiences. Happy times, good times, difficult times, times of sorrow. They are all part of the ebb and flow in life's development. Although we probably all wish for only the good times, the difficult times often provide the greatest catalysts for change, for growth. During the good times, when we feel like we are riding the crest of a wave, it is easy for us to become contended or complacent with our lives.

Then we begin to atrophy, our growth stops, all circuits of life start to slowly close down. Like a muscle that has not been used, complacency leads to narrowness of vision, a restriction of bodily functions, and a contraction of life itself. So that life becomes like Beckett's characters in "Waiting for Godot"—a tedious wait for some Messiah of Savior, a wait that never ends, until the end at death. Not much of a life; not a life worth living.

Friction provides a dynamic energy. It breaks the inertia of set patterns, challenges accepted ways, demands new methods and innovative approaches. It is during the phases of friction in our lives that we are forced to make resolutions.

Our life, our very existence on plant Earth is a series of

conflicts needing to be resolved. The duration of these conflicts depends upon our awareness, upon our desire to learn and grow.

We stand on the threshold of great wisdom. However, we must open our eyes if we are to see. We open our eyes when we start to look inward. Not on an egotistical, personality level, but rather when we start to look at who we truly are. SELF REVELATION IS THE TRUE RELIGION.

The religious teachings, as they are expressed today, have forgotten this very key point. Instead, today's religious institutions purport the coming of a Messiah, a wonder person to take away all our sins, a magic elixir, by which we become perfected by someone else doing it for us.

Do you believe that's the way? It is not. The way to heaven is a journey of self-discovery, a self-revelation that comes through learning more about ourselves, a learning that takes place in the various experiences of life.

The two BIG questions you will be asked when this life's work is done are: WHAT HAVE YOU LEARNED AND WHOM HAVE YOU HELPED. Ask yourself those questions right now and answer them honestly. Then see where you are, what you have been doing, and in what direction you are going.

When you become consciously aware of the lessons you have learned and, as importantly, the lessons you have yet to learn, you come to a realization that life is a progression of steps through expanding awareness, opening the consciousness to self-revelation, and self-discovery. Whom have you helped? Think about it. We will discuss this in greater length in the forthcoming pages, but for now, seed your conscience with these questions.

No matter what you are doing in your life, you have reached a point where self-discovery is becoming more and more important for you. Look for it in your life. Right now. See where you could be manifesting the wonders of self-discovery. It may be subtle. It may be something you consider insignificant. Maybe it is as simple as your reacting differently to a situation that, two months ago, you might have reacted to more negatively (self-destructive). It may seem insignificant, but it is not.

On your journey to true understanding, you will find that the spiritual urge is the most powerful driving force in the world.

Why? Because it is a force that is in complete harmony with the procession of life. Life is evolving in spiritual understanding. The urge is in sync with the unfolding of life, not in friction with life which can be wearying.

As Luke Skywalker was told in the Star War Trilogy, "MAY THE FORCE BE WITH YOU!"

And guess what? It is. To be aware of this force, this energy of the spiritual urge, all you have to do is tap into it. How? First, let go of all your preconceptions, your assumptions, judgments and opinions of reality. Instead of maintaining a running commentary on life's actions and reactions, let go and live life. Live it with an openness, with no expectations, but with the awe of a child discovering a new world for the first time.

It is a unique experience, one we have forgotten. By ridding ourselves of expectations, we allow ourselves to *experience* life. Truly experience it. Expectations place conditions on our experiences.

Think about it. Think about the times when you last planned some event or activity. Did you have certain expectations about it? Were those expectations fulfilled? Were you disappointed?

Now think about the times when you did something spontaneously. Wasn't there more of a sense of excitement, of adventure? When we free ourselves from our limited expectations and conditions, we open ourselves up to life and to living.

Unconditional Love Is The Highest Form Of Service

By giving unconditional love, you free yourself from the slavery of expectations, of rigid limitations. When I say unconditional love, I do not mean solely in your interactions with other people. I also mean giving unconditional love to you, yourself.

Do you love yourself? Oh, I do not mean in a narcissistic manner of loving how you appear. I mean do you truly love yourself? So few people today really do. Why? Because of the conditions they place upon themselves. The expectations that tell us "Yes, indeed, I *could* love myself, IF…."

"IF" — the response of the conditional world. Eliminate the "IF's" in your life when it comes to love. You will find it is easier to love. It is easier to live. Unconditional love is giving back to the world. It is also a magical tonic. If you will love your conditions in life, you change the conditions. Love your environment, and you change the environment. Love yourself, and you change the world.

Needs and Wants

What do you need? What do you want? Although some people may think the difference between these two questions is merely a matter of semantic quibbling, there is a profound difference between needs and wants.

We attract experiences, the lessons in events, to ourselves by our needs. What are our needs? Do we really need anything in this life? Do we need that racy sports car? Do we need that person in our life? Needing is a rather negative energy, because it indicates a sense of dependency.

Wants, wanting, are a more positive force, for there isn't the urgency (or the condition) of dependency. Ask yourself, do you want that person in your life? Or do you need him? Do you need to see that movie someone recommended, or do you want to see it? Do you want to eat that piece of cheesecake, or do you need to eat it?

There are no needs

If you can become firm in your convictions, you will understand what I mean. The difference between the needs and the wants in your life is essential in your growing awareness.

"I don't need someone in my life as a relationship. I want to have a successful relationship. I want love in my life. I want to eat to live. I want a good education. I want a good job. I want good health. I want a lot of things. But do I need them? Do I truly need them?" NO.

Perhaps we were taught that to want too much is to be

26

greedy. Do you believe that?

If you do, please see that you are looking at life as a fixed commodity — only so much to go around. Yet, life is filled with abundance, not with a lack of it.

The only limits are those we place upon ourselves. Self-imposed limitations manifest from a sense of need.

Whatever we worship, we attract. If you worship "I can't", then "can't" is what you will receive. If you worship lack, then lack is your reward. If you worship limitations, then limitations are your experience. If you give your love conditionally, then you will receive love on condition.

Please realize that when you give hate, you get hate in return. When you give anger, you will get anger. When you give negativity, you get negativity.

It was while in England near Stonehenge that the author had his first encounter with UFOs and their occupants. These experiences will be described in a future volume.

What Goes Around, Comes Around

Give love, and you will get love. Give love unconditionally and you get unconditional love.... from the Universe. In the Universe, there is no condemnation of us for our actions. It is only man who becomes the judge, jury and executioner to his own thinking.

As a man thinks, so shall he become. Thoughts are energy, like everything else. Your thoughts constantly are being broadcast. Whatever you are thinking about right now is being broadcast out. And there will always be someone out there picking up those transmissions of yours. Whatever thoughts you are sending out, you are going to receive the same sort of thoughts back.

Like always attracts like

If you send out hostile energy to a negative situation, you feed that situation. By feeding it, all that negative energy comes back to you. And it comes back manyfold. You are likely to become depressed, angry, frustrated.

If this continues over time, your thinking is likely to affect your physical condition. Illness will follow, for dis-ease and dis-harmony lead to disease and illness. Do you want to be sick? Do you want to have nothing or no one in your life? Do you worship lack?

These are some of the questions each of us must really ask ourselves. What do you want?

If you feel caught in a trap, give yourself permission to spring the trap. If you feel there is no way out, reach inward and upward toward the higher forces, the divine spark in each of us waiting to ignite. You are the torchbearer. You are the one who will light that flame to burn brilliantly. Just give yourself permission to do so. Allow yourself to change. Give yourself permission for the things you want out of life.

Can you? Will you?

Sometimes we step back from ourselves, look at ourselves and with all the objectivity of a need masquerading as a want, we say we could, if we were not such a "bad" person. What?! Our lives would be turned around, if what? If the conditions were met. What conditions? Whatever conditions we devise to limit ourselves.

One of the most effectively designed conditions for keeping us from change is self-recrimination — the expectation we have not met, the success we have not achieved, the condition by which we can love ourselves. LOVE YOURSELF UNCONDITIONALLY.

Today, right now, at this very moment, forgive yourself for any guilt, fear or sin you may harbor about yourself. For they are the conditions that hold you back. By forgiving yourself, you slay the dragon within. You cut the anchor cords of negativity, getting rid of dis-ease. By forgiving ourselves for what we consider to be transgressions, we are cleaning the temple, the sanctity of GOD in the image and form of mankind. By so doing, we put ourselves in touch with our higher self, where the spirit of truth dwells.

Wisdom in action is forgiveness and unconditional love

Just for a moment, reflect on your relationship with your parents. Do you love your parents? Do you hate them? Do you blame them for the way your life is now? Do you judge them? However you might answer these questions, one question is paramount: CAN YOU FORGIVE THEM?

If you love your parents, there is no need for forgiveness. However, that type of relationship with parents is not universal.

29

Some of us feel anger or frustration over our relationship with our parents. But do we see clearly? Often, we get so caught up in a situation that we tend to see it solely from our own perspective, a perspective of limited self-interest. We see how other people's actions or behavior have had an effect upon us. So it is with our parents.

From the childish perspective that parents are omnipotent and can do no wrong, we forget that parents are people like ourselves, trying to learn their lessons in everyday life, struggling to meet their challenges with their own sets of trials and tribulations.

But we lose sight of that. Instead, some of us are ensnared in the trap that our lives are wrong due to our parents poor job of parenting. Whether such criticism is valid or not, it is still a trap.

If your relationship with your parents has been bad, ask yourself whether you have made resolution with it, with them? If you have not made resolution, recognize that you are holding on to a feeling, a negative feeling, that is only blocking your own growth, your own fulfillment.

Therefore, eliminate those feelings. How? First, by forgiving yourself.

"Forgive myself?" you may ask incredulously. Why should I forgive myself when it is them, my parents, who have done wrong? I am the one wronged, the victim. The role of victim, the idea of being victimized, is a trap, a severely limiting trap. If you want to move on from these limitations, from the bindings that hold you back, indeed forgive yourself for holding such thoughts.

Once you have done this, then forgive them. Can you? Will you?

Perhaps it might help if you remember a master's words: "Forgive them, for they know not what they do". If you can forgive them, then move to a point where you can send them unconditional love. Love, unconditional love, is a power that unleashes the abundance in your life.

The Bird That Flies Highest Sees The Furthest

By ridding your mind and emotions of all negative clutter, you raise your consciousness. Upward, toward the light, in the warming comfort of unconditional love. But first you must risk everything like the little bird leaving its nest to fly. You must be willing to launch yourself from your morass of preconceived opinions and habitual response patterns. That is the true alchemy of turning base metal into gold. It is the flight of the phoenix. If you will do that, dear friend, then you will soar on high.

It is a marvelous feeling. For you will find that your perceptions, both inner and outer, are clearer and made more manifest. What we term psychic abilities will become more evident within you. And these abilities will enhance the awareness of your spiritual progression in life.

It is like being in a helicopter. If you are caught in the gridlock of a traffic jam, you can't see what is causing the bottleneck. But if you are in a helicopter, above the traffic jam, you see what is causing it, where the flow is blocked.

The same is true in your development. Perhaps you may feel, or think, that I have laid certain traps for you. You may consider my suggestions as possible only for applicants to sainthood. They are not.

One of the beauties of growth, of self-development, is the unfolding process, whereby certain talents or qualities are revealed and made manifest as your progress. It is like the unfolding of a flower bud into full bloom.

People on the path are very evident to each other. Not so much by their actions or what they might say, but more importantly by their manner. As you develop, as you progress in your own unfolding, you will find it easier and easier to love. A child-like awe of life resurfaces, a clear perception that regenerates your very being, manifesting itself externally as a certain calm to your presence.

Self-growth will come to all of us. It is a question of time and nourishment.

It will come to you. The turning point, as I have mentioned before, will come at the appropriate time. No sooner, no later. It may come in those "healing crises" that occur periodically in our lives to catalyze us into transformations along the way. It may come quietly in the night while you sleep. But it will come to you. In time.

Through awareness, commitment and understanding you can nourish your own growth. The moment we acknowledge life as a process of evolution, we take on added responsibilities. The power of transformation. We work with it every day. Sometimes unconsciously, with possibly dire consequences.

George Orwell is quoted as saying that a person gets the face they deserve by age 52. What he meant was that as we are, so we become. Indelibly etched by that age on our faces, as though chiseled in stone, is the mark of our character, our qualities, our being.

You have seen it. You may have seen it in a person who looks incredibly angry, or seen bitterness scrawled in the lines of a face.

Distorted thoughts create a distorted body. Wrong thinking can and does take its toll. Wrong thinking and negative emotions lead to distress, dis-ease, and dis-harmony. In turn, they create a diseased body.

It does not have to be that way. Do you know that the greatest diet, the greatest body health technique is not some specific exercise program, or a calculated food intake program? It is the mind. The power of the mind is the germinating ground for our later creations. We must protect it at all costs.

If you truly want to be one of the "beautiful people" (in the true sense of the word), then work on your mind. Re-educate yourself. Program yourself to snip all those negative thoughts to which you give form. And instead, tune your mind to the higher self, to the understanding of your life. In so doing, you will be able to forgive, to love unconditionally, to share and help others, no matter who they might be. Even strangers.

The author shown in "earlier days" at the microphone in New York City where he worked as a disc jockey and talk show host on various radio stations.

Heaven and Hell

Heaven and hell are not places, no matter what you have been taught. You can't drive to heaven. You can't catch a plane to hell, no matter what people might say. Why not try it?

But you can still get to heaven, or you can go to hell. But they are not places, not physical locales. They are states—states of mind. Consciousness or unconsciousness.

Hell is darkness. It is those areas of life we do not understand that are negative. We are all plunged into darkness in this material world. It is done with clear intent and many guideposts along the way. It is done so that we, as individuals, can find the light, attain our own enlightened-ness, enlightenment.

This analogy is repeated throughout man's history and legends. We see the fall from grace in the Bible with the expulsion of Adam and Eve from the Garden of Eden. It is repeated in the tarot system with the Fall of the Fool, and in the cabalistic system, at the crossing of the abyss.

It is the alchemy of spiritual essence into material form. But in the darkness of matter, that spiritual essence yearns to rediscover its true heritage. And the process ensues. The individual starts to seek answers. He does so in time, for there is much of it. He goes on many journeys, through countless experiences, in myriads of relationships and entanglements.

As he goes through life cycles, the individual learns about living. He begins to realize why he is here. And then he develops what he has been given to work with. Eventually, he reaches understanding, and attunement.

One of the beauties of life is that it is all about cycles. We know some of these cycles: cycles of existence—birth—life—death; cycles of earth parameters—day and night, the four seasons; cycles of physical life—youth—adult—age.

Perhaps we are not aware enough of the latter cycle, the cycle of physical life. It is hard for a young person to see the reality of an older person's perspective. And in reflection, older people look at the young and say that youth is wasted on the young.

Yet in the past few years, various popular culture books have come out, focusing on certain "crisis" periods in an individual's life. But depicting them in terms of "crises" is to forget the valuable opportunity and potential for sharp transitioning during these times.

Chronologically through life, we go through various cycles. These cycles are broken down into different phases—times when we are learning about specific areas or a certain function. FOR EVERYTHING THERE IS A SEASON, AND A TIME TO EVERY PURPOSE UNDER THE HEAVENS.

Our human life is broken into three cycles that have a 27 to 30 year duration each. Back in the 1960's, student radicals on college campuses proclaimed that you could not trust anyone over the age of thirty. It is ironic that the students were unaware of a profound truth.

Those of you who have passed that time in your life, reflect and remember how that period was a time of tying up loose ends, of going back over certain things that had occurred during your life.

Maybe you remember reconnecting with people from whom you had not heard for a long stretch of time. Maybe you experienced a breakup, or more responsibility, or a feeling of weightiness. Whatever you may have experienced, this period was a time of strong transitioning for you, a maturation that changed you significantly.

That time frame is the time when we move from adolescence and become an adult, true adulthood. As we enter our thirties, we are moving through the period where we take on our life's purpose in work. This is our productive cycle, where we work in the world, sow our fields, no matter what type of function we may have.

At the age of 57 to 60, we go through another significant transition. It is a time of resolving, and coming to terms with any loose ends of the past 27 to 30 years.

Those of you who have passed this mark may remember it as a sense of diminishing physical capabilities, a sense of age creeping up on you. Death, the prospect of mortality, seems to loom during this time, for there is an awareness that the person's productive years are drawing to a close. However, with this transitioning period, there is another significant change, a time of moving from the productive cycle of one's life into the harvest period, the third and last cycle in an individual's life.

The harvest period in a person's life is a phase where the spirit in man really comes consciously forward. We see respect for this cycle in the oriental tradition, where older people are venerated and respected for their wisdom and understanding. In societies that are youth-oriented or concerned solely with productivity, this third cycle is often relegated to merely waiting for death.

If we could be aware of these three cycles in our lives, we could then live our lives in accord with the purpose and function of those different phases.

While our lives can be broken up into three major cycles, there are also seven year cycles in our lives.

We have heard the phrase the "seven-year itch." By that phrase alone, there is a connotation of change nagging to be fulfilled.

The Seven Year Cycles In A Human's Life

AGE 0 TO 7: The incarnating soul is still very much connected with the essence of life. This can show itself in many ways. It can manifest as the wonder in experiencing life, the reverential awe of childhood innocence, similar to the biblical parable: Until we become like little children.

The individual in this stage is "en rapport" with mother nature. This rapport may manifest as an ability to perceive nature sprites, elves, or other ethereal forms, and may include imaginary friends.

This first cycle of seven years in human life is the process of the soul incarnating into human form. It is the time in which the child grows physically, his skeletal structure becoming less malleable, more solid in form. It is also the time during which the incarnating soul, its essential quality, is buried by the fall into human personality, the ego quality. The child is conditioned to life by his parents, peers and pedagogues. The child takes on a personality.

AGE 7 TO 14: The emerging ego personality starts to express itself. This is a time when the individual develops his creative self-assertion. No longer content to adopt the ways of parents and society, the child speaks now in terms of "I." It is the time in which the child begins to challenge the limitations others would try to place on him.

It is also a time of challenge in physical terms, as the child grows into his physical body. In the child's play there is an element of risk-taking, whatever form it might take. Increasingly, a sense of personal power develops as the child takes on the growth of his physical body along with the strengthening of his ego personality. This is the period of clarion call to creative self-assertion: I AM SOMEONE.

AGE 14 TO 21: As the child becomes aware of a power of procreation with the new-found sexual energy through the crisis of puberty, a differentiation occurs: It is during this period in time when the individual consciously begins to separate himself from the father and mother figures. There is a recognition that the father and mother are not Gods, infallible in their decisions, looked up to for sustenance. Rather, the parents are seen as human, liable to make mistakes, prone to errors of judgement.

The individual now begins to readjust himself for relationships. While this period incorporates a differentiation between the young adolescent and his parents, there is a seeking-out of peer relationships, relationships that now also encompass sexual relationships.

In relating to others, there is now a honing of the creative self-assertion developed during the preceding seven year cycle. Now, we look to how our actions impact upon others.

No longer just the "I AM" expression, but self-expression in relating with others. It is during this time that the individual begins to question society's terms of relating to one another. It is during this age when the individual works on a social conscience.

AGE 21 TO 28: During this time, the individual moves further away from parental and educational conditioning. The individual is ready to take a personal stand in the world. This is the time when the individual moves from learning to applying. The individual is likely to finish formalized educational studies, and may move out of the parental nest. During this time, the individual is likely to take on a job, live on his own, perhaps marry and begin his own family.

This is the last quarter in the first cycle of adolescence. It is during this phase that the person consciously starts to move into his own life function and system.

AGE 28 TO 35: With the beginning of the individual's cycle of productivity at this age, the purpose now is to express his true individuality. Up to this point, life had been lived in assimilating and living one's life for the past conditioning to cultural parameters. The testing of the waters in self-expression may have been tried prior to this phase, but such attempts were likely to have been strongly influenced by past culture and family considerations. It is at this phase that the maturation of the individual takes place and he accepts responsibility for his actions as an individual.

This is a time of rebirth, with associated labor pains. This rebirth is the maturation of the adolescent into an adult. As an adult, family matters — not the parental family but the family created by choice — become of paramount concern.

AGE 35 TO 42: At this stage in his development, the person seeks to express his true individuality in the various areas of family, business, religion and community involvement. This is a time of self-awareness, when the person can realize that he does have choice in his actions. Of course, with choice comes responsibility. And during this stage, the responsibility is to be true to one's self.

While the self-determining individuality is struggling for prominence, the reaction by external forces, past conditioning and patterns, can be one of opposition.

Not only does the individual struggle against the tentacles of past actions and entanglements, but there comes a growing awareness of the polarities between his own internal and external forces. Through the synthesis of these two forces, the person has the opportunity to bring about an integration of self-individuality.

Should the opportunity for awareness and self-integration be lost during this phase, then the individual will face the succeeding "mid-life" period as one fraught with crisis and chaos.

AGE 42 TO 49: The mid-life period is a dramatic shifting of gears. At this time in life the individual becomes aware that his external being—his physical body—is in a state of decline. The process of aging becomes apparent, as the parents' generation dies away, and this age group takes their parents place as the "older" generation.

People often rebel against change. They do so from anxiety, spurred on by a sense that life is fast ticking away, and that this is their last chance. As a result, this can be a time when people try to recapture their youth. Some may change their clothing styles to a younger fashion, others become involved with a new romantic partner.

While the physical prowess begins to decline at this stage, this is also the time when the inner forces—the internal being— become more developed. This is the changing of gears. Instead of being solely concerned with grabbing the gusto from life's experiences, the person becomes more reflective regarding the meaning behind events. It is the time when we can become more aware of the spiritual side to ourselves. It is a time when we are better able to see the spirit in matter. But, of course, we must look in order to see.

AGE 49 TO 56: From learning through experience, we gain wisdom. This wisdom is to be shared. This period is a phase of positive expression, of giving back what one has learned. This may incorporate increased social responsibility or the education of others.

From the preceding seven-year cycle, we have touched base with a sense of lack, of failure, of mortality. Yet, if that period has been used constructively, there has also been a regeneration whereby the individual is now concerned with a new quality in his life — spirit.

This seven year cycle is the final quadrant of the productive cycle. As we pass through this cycle, we are moving toward the harvest period, which can include retirement from the productive function. As if in preparation for that major change, the individual now seeks something beyond mere productivity. He seeks the quality of wisdom.

AGE 56 TO 63: During this period, the individual transitions from the second life cycle of productivity into the third, the harvest cycle. During this phase, we begin to reap what we have sown during the past 30 odd years.

Another chance at rebirth is possible at this time. Now the rebirth is from an adult human personality into a spiritual re-polarization. For this is a time of review and reassessment of what is important, what is essential to life. Not so much life in terms of the individual personality but life in terms of the collective. This is the age for philosophy.

The montage of experiences are seen more clearly for their undercurrents of lessons and purpose behind the events. It is this understanding that can impinge upon the collective conscious-ness at this time.

AGE 63 TO 70: This seven-year cycle sees a preparation for the after-life. Either this is done consciously by the individual who opens himself up to new realms of consciousness, and radi-ates wisdom of the developing spirit, or it is done unconsciously by the individual who becomes bored, listless, and merely waiting for death.

These are the various functions and purposes of each seven-year cycle up to the age of seventy. During these age periods, cer-tain opportunities and specific challenges are provided for us. If we are aware of the meaning of these various cycles, then we can live in sync with the chronological evolution in man. Unaware of these different cycles, and we are apt to go through life banging our heads again walls, feeling frustrated and daunted at every turn. But it does not have to be that way.

As we noted in the seven-year cycles in man's life, human life evolves from the physical to the spiritual. In this process, that which is not essential drops away. It is all part of the soul's pro-gression.

The journey we embark on in life is filled with pain, sadness, emotional chaos, frustrations, rejections.... EVERYTHING YOU HAVE TO MASTER WITHIN YOURSELF.

While we are subjected to challenges, we are also provided opportunities. The opportunity to live our life filled with joy, health, understanding, success, happiness, LOVE. The choice is ours. Individually, yours and mine. When we start to place more

41

VALUE on the spirit than on matter, we turn our lives around. A resurrection takes place, as glorious as the mystery of Golgotha where the spirit in CHRIST gains victory over the crush of matters.

It will happen to all of us. Eventually. By increasing our awareness, however, we can quicken the process. By making right choices, we accelerate our evolution.

One such choice is in the right action of mind. Our mind is a powerful tool. It creates our future. What we visualize in our mind we project into our conditions. The power of mind over matter, the power of positive thinking, reflect the laser quality of our mind stuff.

Too often, however, we let our mind wreak havoc in our lives. One way we do so is by worrying about possible future situations, mulling them over to the point where every calamity and catastrophe imagineable has been built into that future condition. Or we set ourselves up. We start on a project with enthusiasm and zest. But when we face any form of resistance, any obstacle or obstruction to the completion of our project, we start to question whether we can actually pull it off.

From where do these worries and concerns come? They come from insecurity.... an insecurity about our self. Some of these insecurities have been programmed into our minds from past conditioning, past incidents. These programs are like tape loops that repeatedly condition our attitudes and affect our behavior.

Because these tape loops have played for such a long time, we have come to rely upon them. Rely upon them to prevent ourselves from getting what we want. Rely upon them to engrain a sense of lack and limitation in our lives. Rely upon them to provide us with yet another example of our failure. Some reliance! What a dependency!

Although these tape loops may have become dominant as an instinctual response pattern, you can loosen their grip. Even cut their hold upon your behavior and actions. How?

First, through awareness. How aware are you of your actions? When you do something, even routine tasks, do you just go through the motions? That is, is it mechanical? Is your life mechanical, the same drudgery and routine, day in, day out?

Remember the parable: Until you become like a little child, with awe and wonder about life, you will be locked into the same tape loops, the same programs of frustrations and self-defeat. It does not have to be that way.

By awareness of your actions, you can begin to see some of the tape loops in operation. Once you see what is going on, you can then initiate right action. What kind of action? Modifying your behavior. Perhaps only in reflection at first. THE MORE YOU BECOME AWARE OF WHAT YOU DO AND HOW YOU DO IT, THE MORE CONSCIOUS YOU BECOME OF WHY YOU DO IT

If the effects are self-defeating, you can change them. Maybe slowly at first. That's OK. Rome was not built in a day. Nor is our evolution and development through life done in one day, or even in one lifetime. It takes time. Just by starting you put into process your conscious evolution, a concentration on your own growth.

Similar to your experiences, my life has been a series of unusual events. Yet, as I began to look, I started to see how each event gave me a deeper insight about myself and my direction in this period. OUR LIVES ARE OUR GREATEST TEACHERS.

We sometimes forget this. Occasionally, when we have had some remarkable insight into our own lives, we assume it to be a universal truth, readily accepted by others. And so we spread the word. With our new insight, we go out and try to save the world. We bang on people's doors, trying to wake them from their stupor. There is an obnoxious enthusiasm that often overcomes people when they "get religion." It is a righteousness that is blind to where other people are in their lives, in their consciousness, in their understanding.

Before *you* go out and save the world, SAVE THE WORLD WITHIN YOURSELF FIRST.

By your example, you can affect multitudes. Like a pebble dropped into a pond, your growing spurts through life will have an effect upon others. Let your light shine brightly, and others will see you as a beacon.

THE DRUID PRAYER

GRANT OH GOD THEY PROTECTION
AND IN PROTECTION—STRENGTH!
AND IN STRENGTH—UNDERSTANDING!
AND IN UNDERSTANDING—KNOWLEDGE!
AND IN KNOWLEDGE—THE KNOWLEDGE OF
    JUSTICE!
AND IN THE KNOWLEDGE OF JUSTICE—THE LOVE
    OF IT:
AND IN THE LOVE OF IT—THE LOVE OF ALL
    EXISTENCES:
AND IN THE LOVE OF ALL EXISTENCES—THE LOVE
    OF GOD AND ALL GOODNESS

The Magus

Do you believe in magic? What is magic? Is it a series of deceptions or sleight-of-hand? Is it tricks perpetrated on the limitations of our sense faculties? Or is magic something else?

To me, there is magic in seeing a butterfly soar after crawling as a caterpillar. I feel magic when I have a client open himself up to be healed, and has healed himself. I sense magic in watching a baby grow into childhood, then adolescent into adulthood and maturity into old age.

For me, magic is a state of change. A transformation—whether it be physical, mental, or emotional. Our world is filled with magic. If you will only believe it.

Can you believe in magic? Do you believe that you could be a master magician? You can.

Magic is in knowing you can change, if you want to change. Give yourself permission to change. That's a start. For then you begin to look beyond the routine drudgery and begin to see what is beyond. You go beyond the limitations and look to the possibilities.

Chance starts with desire.

What do you want? Whatever it might be, focus your energies on it, without wavering in your pursuit, and you will get it. Can you believe that? If you can, you are ready to take your role as the magus and like a master magician transform your life from lacks and limitations into growth and abundance.

That is the greatest act of magic we can perform. Transmuting the base metal of our character into the radiant gold of divinity. It is perfection; paradise. It is divine.

45

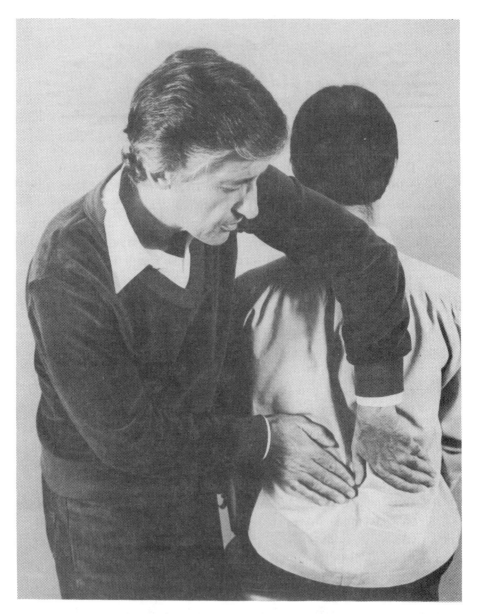

The author shown demonstrating his special healing techniques as described in the pages of this book.

The God Within

If GOD really wanted a place to hide, where would GOD hide? Within man. For that would be the last place man would look for GOD. Despite all the teachings to the contrary, man still refuses to accept his heritage as the son of GOD. With man's fall from grace, when the essence goes within the ego of the growing child as he takes on personality around the age of seven, man loses the clear perceptions of reality to society's accepted illusions in mere appearances.

As the natural communion with life ends so, too, does man's connection to the continual progression, and evolution, in the life cycle. Look around you and see how man treats *himself*. Man's physical body is in disrepair, the temple of GOD ill treated by rampant negative thought forms, emotional chaos and self-destructive indulgence. As we think, so shall we become.

As we look around at the state of mankind today, it is obvious what we have become. As though caught in some carnival fun house with distorted mirrors, we see etched upon every human being his emotions, his qualities and his character. There is sadness, bitterness, anger and defeat displayed during these times. The lack of connection to the divine force that lies waiting to be ignited within each of us has sewn seeds of personal discontent, hostility and aggression.

Yet having torn down this physical temple, we seek to build it up. True to Western civilization, we do so by looking at the symptoms and not at the essential cause. And, thus, we repair not our emotions and the negative tape loops running constantly in our minds. Rather, we repair ourselves by cosmetic approaches — facial applications, plastic surgery, jewels and costumes. And we become the beautiful people.

The irony of it. For beauty is not the momentary bloom, or a transitory blossom. Beauty is the entire process of being, in which that momentary bloom is but a phase. And beauty comes not from application. It radiates out with life, love and character.

If you seek to be beautiful, to allow the fullness of life into your own life, cosmetic means may get you a brief hit, or two, but it will be momentary. To truly find, one must search. Not the far corners of the earth. It is not even necessary to get out of your chair. For the search is a journey within....

The moment you truly reach inward and upward for the highest within yourself, your physiological appearance will change. Our external appearance is a reflection of our inner being. If we are confused, chaotic and angry within ourselves, no amount of beauty creams or cosmetics will effectively mask our expression of discontent.

Do you want to be beautiful? Then clean up your act. See yourself as you are. Not your opinion about yourself, or other people's opinions. See yourself as part of it all. As part of divinity. For you are.

REALITY FOLLOWS BELIEF. Which came first, the chicken or the egg? The law of cause and effect is everywhere. It is part of the life process. The transformation of the driving force into forms that continually change. CHANGE. Can you?

REALITY FOLLOWS BELIEF. It bears repeating, for we continually do so. Unfortunately, we do so unconsciously, thereby caroming back and forth between emotional crises and negative conditions. YOUR THOUGHTS CREATE YOUR CONDITIONS.

Think negatively, think in a mindset of lacks and unfulfilled wishes, and you will create such conditions. Negative thoughts breed negative conditions.

However, if you see yourself as part of it all — part of the process, of this divine plan — then you are less likely to tap into your own personal ego conditioning tape loops that might set you up and cause you to fail.

It takes time. It takes awareness. Similar to any birthing process, it needs constant nourishment and focused awareness. Nourishment in the process of the creative self-expression of the individuality, YOUR GROWTH, takes many forms. It comes through books or discussions like this. It comes through a diet that is concerned with nutrition. It comes through our lessons learned in the natural procession of life. It comes from a respect for ourselves as part of the GOD force. It comes through a life cycle that is more inherently in tune with the cosmic rhythms. The tidal action of the oceans, night into day, rest into action, breathing in and breathing out.

How well do you breathe? Peculiar question? Not really. But possibly one you have not thought of for some time, if at all. Why? Because we take breathing for granted. It is automatic. It comes naturally. We do it all the time.

We had better. Otherwise, we would be dead. Man can go three weeks without food before he dies. He can go three days without water before he dies. But man can go only three minutes without breathing before he dies.

Breath is life. Later, we will discuss several techniques to increase the awareness and proper rhythm for our breathing. Right now, recognize breathing as essential, even though it is automatic. And try to focus on your breathing more and more. For inhaling nourishes our body, and vitalizes our blood stream. Exhaling allows us to release the toxins, the waste matter within our bodies.

You know how people sometimes refer to those who are going through senility as not getting enough oxygen to the brain. Breath is indeed life. The Hindus talk of "prana", the life force contained within the air, invisible to our normal sight perceptions. By inhaling, we take this life force into ourselves. That is why awareness and proper breathing are so essential. It affects our brain. It affects our thoughts. It affects our life conditions.

You will see. The more you put into practice some of our insights and techniques given here, the more you will discover.

You do not have to find some authoritative regimen to implement these understandings and applications. Really, it is not necessary. Just do it naturally. Like the awe of a little child at some new insight or flash that comes to you.

If you will look at your life, at the lives of people around you, and look objectively, not with judgement or opinion, you are likely to see how much each of us has to put up with every day.

In our day and age, with its fast pace and high technology, we are being asked to master more and more situations in different areas of our lives in a much faster time frame. Think about it.

Those of you who have experienced some of this life may be able to see how life has accelerated in the last five to ten years. We are being asked to master financial survival, relationships, parenting, at a quicker pace and with a large degree of uncertainty and anxiety in the air.

There is a Chinese proverb, some would say a curse, that goes: "May you live in interesting times."

Indeed, we do. These times are times that try man's soul and press mankind to the very limits of its resilience. But these are also times that allow us to make quantum leaps in our understanding, in our consciousness, in our evolution.

A quickening is taking place. Not only in the life of collective mankind, but in our individual lives as well. For the life of the collective is a reflection of the multitude of individual lives being lived.

If mankind is at war, and at present over one quarter of the world's countries are currently involved in war, then it is only a reflection of the war within the self of the individual lives. We are at war within ourselves. Our personal conflicts, the petty and trivial becoming paramount, are manifestations of our confusion, our ignorance. Did someone really say that ignorance is bliss?

While war rages, both on the external level and the internal, we can go forth as crusaders. First, begin to re-evaluate who you are and what you are.

Is there a war raging within you? Are there the vestiges of a brushfire deep within your soul that threaten to flare up? Do you have personal conflicts to resolve? Can you see the direction in which you are heading? The direction you want to go in? Do you know who you are? And what you are here to do?

You know the answer to all of these questions, and any others that may be nagging within your mind. They are within you. They are not the conditioning from your parents or society. They are that true you. Your true individuality to be expressed in a creative manner. How? No one can give you the answer, EXCEPT yourself. You know that answer. And you will learn it, if you have forgotten, by listening to that small voice within. It knows. You know.

Like the biblical allegory of the prodigal son, we too lose our way. We forget what we are looking for. We ignore the process of evolution in its metronome-like swings between ever lessening extremes. That's why books like these are written. As guides along the way.

In your journey through life, hold strong to the process of mankind made in the image of GOD, preserving and mastering through the experiences of earth life, to realize the GOD force within yourself. WE ARE ALL GODS IN THE MAKING.

Every one of us. Each of us is part of a great master plan. We may often swear that the chaos of "random" incidents defies any sort of plan, much less a master plan. But that occurs through a narrowing of our perspective, when we look only at a small piece in the larger puzzle and lose sight of the total picture.

Man's knowledge is an extension of his consciousness. We mentioned it before: reality follows belief. There are no limits to mankind's expansion in understanding, only the capacity to which man is open to new insights, new understanding, even when they may be radical departures from previous beliefs and standards.

If we keep in sight the total picture, the total process of development and evolvement, we shall see the grand design in all its intricate workings.

To me, one of the most beautiful sights in the cycles of life is that of a tree. For it encompasses and displays the multi-faceted aspects of life. From an acorn a mighty oak is grown. Indeed. A seed dropped, perhaps born by the wind to a distant spot, out from the shadow of the mother oak. The seed held gently by the earth, nourished in the darkness by the moist soil. To sprout and grow toward the light.

This tiny shoot grows through seasonal experiences, each year getting bigger and stronger. The tree grows up, becomes taller and starts to take on branches. The tree grows out. The once spindly little trunk standing majestically strong. The winds of change constantly blow through the tree limbs.

Rains come, provide water to nourish the tree. The tree continues to develop. As it grows, it goes through basic seasonal changes. In the Spring, the tree's limbs sprout tiny tight-closed buds that later break forth as the foliage of late Spring, Summer and early Fall. Come Fall and the tree loses its leaves in a radiant display of color, to stand apparently lifeless through the winter.

Continuously it grows upward and develops outward. If we look at the cycle of a tree, it provides incredible symbolism to the process of life and living. And it records that process. Every year the tree in its widening breadth takes on another ring in its trunk, a wisdom ring which records the conditions of growth during that year.

While we might assume the tree stands alone, there is a larger picture to the puzzle. Not only does the tree provide us with the analogy of growth, a tree may serve many functions. Tree limbs provide nestings for birds. The oak provides acorns for squirrels. In summer, a leafy tree offers shade from the sun's heat. The wood of a tree gives us building materials for houses, provides us with wood for fires. Fallen leaves decay and become a mulch to revitalize the soil from which it sprang.

The interweaving and interdependency in life is a majestic spectacle. Perhaps part of its majesty stems from the fact that too often we tend to neglect the process and look only at one piece.

Do that and you are likely to lose sight of the total picture, and some of the opportunities contained therein. Mother nature provides us with many lessons about living and progression. It is a question of looking, of listening, of being en rapport with nature.

At the turn of the century there lived a black man, born into slavery, who grew into a true individual whose depth and sensitivity would highlight his contributions to international renown. This man was George Washington Carver, truly a gentle man. His spiritual communion with nature is legendary. He would communicate with nature, speaking to it, holding it, sensing something in it that others could not sense. And in turn nature made him aware of its limitless abundance and mysteries. Carver called Mother Nature his teacher.

It is one of the best.

And part of that is relationship.

Bryce Bond and his co-host Linda Pelerin reach millions weekly in the metropolitan area with their *Dimensions in Parapsychology* TV program.

Relatedness

Relationships, the act of relating, have become an art in our day and age. For our society reflects an inability to relate. We see it reflected in the divorce statistics, in the singe-parent family structures, in the number of singles who are committed to a singles lifestyle.

Fundamental changes are taking place in the ways we relate to one another. These changes are the result of the present dichotomy in our individual selves. On the one hand, we are evolving as individuals more and more toward self-development and the expression of the true individuality.

On the other hand, the techniques and attitudes of our self-development have subtly contributed to an ego reinforcement of the personal "me," a subtle trap and seduction indeed.

Relationships always have and always will provide us with the important lessons of developing ourselves through the process of interaction with others. It is part of man's life cycle. We see it as the child goes off to school; to learn about himself, than to absorb rote knowledge, through the interaction with his peers.

Relationships start at a very early age. Before birth, the developing human body is completely dependent upon the mother carrying it for life support systems. Dependency continues after birth and throughout childhood. As we grow older, we take on other types of relationships. Not just parent-child relationships, but relationships with friends, relationships with teachers, relationships with the opposite sex. As we move toward maturity, our relationships change.

We have talked repeatedly about change. The same is true in relationships. In your own life, you have probably seen people pass in, through and out of connection with you at various times in your life experience.

Even now, perhaps you find yourself gravitating toward specific new types of people. Maybe some relationships are fading, with certain people moving out of your life.

If there are people from whom you are parting, recognize that it is not because you hate them. It is not because you no longer love them. It is because these people are no longer necessary to your personal growth. Does that sound callous and too full of the "me" attitude? It does not.

We learn through relationships. We come together in dynamic interactions or relationships in order to discover more about ourselves.

When we have learned whatever we can learn from interaction with the other person, we often find the relationship dissolves. Oh, it may do so for various reasons: Death, distant move, lack of continued mutual interests, arguments. Whatever they might be, the real reason that relationships end is because all the lessons to be learned through that other person, at that particular time period and level of development, have been learned. And so, it is time to move on. Whether we so choose, or life conditions insist on it, we move on.

One of the greatest lessons in our interactions with others is to be true to ourselves.

Think about it. Relationships are dynamic interactions of various individuals. In those interactions, however, we too often assume that we must follow the habits and ways of our neighbors and friends. There is almost a silent acquiescence to the standards and conventions of the majority. Otherwise, we are afraid we will be branded as different, that we will become social outcasts.

Think back for a moment. Has there ever been a time when you went along with someone else's idea, even though you thought it was a bad one? Why did you do it? Was it because it was the line of least resistance? Was the social pressure too great to say no? PEER PRESSURE IS ONE OF THE GREATEST TESTS WE CAN MASTER.

Under peer pressure we are likely to do all sorts of things we would not even consider doing if we were alone. There is a blindness to our actions we accept when we acquiesce to peer pressure. It is the blindness of running with the pack. The accepted belief that might makes might and indirectly, somehow, right.

The weight of conventionality has lead us down many a winding road. Conventionality is accepted belief. It is largely based upon the premise that what worked once in the past, will work again now in the present, or even into the future. It is locked into a time frame that may be largely irrelevant to present realities. Yet, hypnotically we accept the idea that what worked in the past will work now as well. It does not always, you know. IN ALL OF LIFE, ESPECIALLY IN RELATIONSHIPS, IT IS ESSENTIAL TO BE TRUE TO YOURSELF.

Some of our relationships take the form of adversity. Relationships, nonetheless, but relationships that provide more an element of frustration, pain, hurt, as opposed to our love relationships, which....

All relationships provide challenges and opportunities

If we are discussing a love relationship, the challenge may be one of possessiveness—love that is conditional, based upon each other's own expectations, and as such limiting to both the people involved. If the relationship is antagonistic, then the opportunity arises to face the conflict not with anger, violence or hate but with awareness and the desire to seek a just resolution.

In relating to others, we get a chance to work out the emotions of our ego. Ego emotions are like heavy anchors. They hold us down. They keep us from truly experiencing or sharing with others. Because of our emotions.

Have you seen love between two people turn sour, even to the point where they manifest hate for each other? It is unfortunate, but it is not a rarity. It is unfortunate because the two people involved are unable to come to terms with the negative emotions that have sprung from a soil once nourished in love.

And what are some of these emotions we have to master in our relationships with other people? Hate, anger, jealousy, fear, animosity, rejection, envy, pride, vanity, unworthiness, ridicule, judgments, and frustrations are some of these emotions.

And each of these emotions is but another anchor to weigh you down, and hold you back from self-mastery through relatedness.

The most powerful force in the universe is love. LOVE IN ACTION manifests GOD on earth.

If you want to clean up your act in your personal relationships, unconditional love is the way. For unconditional love, the ability to love expecting nothing in return, is the highest form of love. It is the love that JESUS taught, when he said to love your brother as yourself.

Loving people unconditionally is to accept them the way they are. Without your conditions, or your expectations, or what you want them to do for you in return.

One of the great clues in relationships is to recognize that we tend to see the other person according to *our* perspective. In looking at someone, we often see only a mirrored image of ourselves. If we happen to see in someone something that we do not like about him, recognize that quite possibly what we are disapproving of is the same quality we do not like about ourselves. Before we judge a person by their actions, question whether those actions seem so dreadful to us because of our own unconscious sense of guilt over similar behavior.

Quite a morass in which we move in our relationships. Quite a mess, one that parallels our present day and age, where we are just incapable of sustaining "good" relationships.

Swell, you might think, disheartened by such a suggestion. So much for a successful relationship. Only found in the pages of romance novels, or on the flickering images of the television screens. Not so.

The fact of the matter is that all we have to do is turn the gears of our behavior patterns. The moment we forgive a person for the faults we imagine they have, and send that person our unconditional love, at that moment, no sooner, no later, we sever the cord of negative emotions toward that person.

Unconditional love is free of judgments. It holds no opinions. It truly wants the very best for an individual, no matter what the personal conflicts are between the two of you. Unconditional love is being able to rejoice in another's success before your own. It is the ability to love a stranger as you do yourself.

LOVE. Love your conditions, and you will change those conditions. Love your environment, and you change that environment. Love yourself, and you change the world.

We change those around us by changing ourselves first. Look not for the change in your brother or sister, look for the change in you. By your changes, you will affect changes in your relationships,in your life, in your loves.

You might argue with this point, and say perhaps that the other person should change his attitude or behavior. And perhaps with your sense of rightness (a. k. a. self-righteousness) you will go forward to change him, correct his ways, in the name of love.

Have you ever thought about the calamities and deaths cause in the name of "love", in the name of "GOD"?

To try and change another, no matter what you use as a rationale, is an ego manipulation. What you are doing is placing conditions on your love. It is the carrot-and-stick routine of relatedness. I will love you more, if you will.... I can't love you, if you won't....

Conditions to our love are restrictions upon our selves. They place limits to our sharing, to our experiencing. Accept people as they are. It is quite a test, no doubt about it. But is essential to be able to do so, before you can truly love the other.

Another master test for all of us is the ability to forgive. It was intoned by the mater JESUS as he hung nailed to the cross when he called out: "Forgive them, for they know not what they do."

It is a powerful affirmation, reinforced by wise understanding. Forgiveness is a phenomenal healing tool. When we are

58

wounded or hurt in our experiences through life, there is the possibility that we might allow that pain to embitter us from similar situations in the future, or even to life itself. You have seen it. Ride a city bus some time, and see the bitterness etched on some faces.

The face is an incredible map. On it becomes etched the life pattern, the individual's reaction to life itself. All kinds of emotions are etched on people's faces. What will you enscrawl upon your own? It is your choice.

In being able to forgive someone, it is not a question of forgive and forget. It is forgiveness and awareness. A dramatic difference.

Forgiveness is letting go of a situation, not holding on to it. It is the recognition that people have to act out their emotional imbalances, coupled with the strength not to get sucked into it. If someone is outlandish in their actions, are we going to match their bizarre behavior?

Are we going to come down to their level and retaliate? If we do, we give that person incredible power over us. For we are reacting in a manner similar to their own. TO THEIR OWN. Important words, for they remind us that everyone of us is a unique individual entity, on various levels of development.

You cannot ask a child of three to have the knowledge of a Nobel physicist in his sixties. You cannot ask of people who know not what they do reason and understanding in their actions, much less so in their interactions.

But can you forgive them? If you can, send them unconditional love. This does not mean you forget, for lessons are to be learned. But if you truly can forgive them, you will feel as if a weight has been lifted from your chest. For indeed a weightiness has. You will have severed the connection to the ego emotion and the negative situation.

Sending unconditional love, like a prayer, will provide the one who hurt us with a healing, and may help him move to a higher understanding. There are many wounded souls out there in the world today. You do not have to be one of them.

There is an old saying that goes: When the student is ready, the teacher appears. It is a very simple but very wise saying. Unfortunately, people tend to believe their teacher is likely to come in raiment of gold cloth, hailed as the Messiah himself. This attitude is akin to the expectant coming in the Jewish religion, and the second coming of the present fundamentalists. If we accept that belief, what happens is that we become like characters out of Beckett's "Waiting For Godot",—waiting expectantly, ever waiting.

Meanwhile, the teacher may have come and gone. WE ARE ALL TEACHERS, WE ARE ALL STUDENTS. As you begin to realize the truth to this statement, you will start to see the varied lessons to be learned in our different relationships.

For that is the importance of relationships: SELF-MASTERY THROUGH RELATEDNESS.

Not everything is black and white. In fact, few things are. Consequently, clear-cut decisions often necessitate weighing of many factors before the actual decision is made. This is also true in our lessons through experience. Often, you won't find your situation or incident clearly marked with the label: "the lesson of this experience is.... "

That is true of all of life. And relationships are no exception.

During moments of floundering, wondering what is the right action, we can go back to the masters, the world teachers who have passed through this life and impacted human culture. No matter what our personal bias or cultural background, the truth is expressed in many forms, in many different manifestations. The teachers are in the multitude. They are the teachers such as JESUS, MOHAMMED, MOSES, CONFUCIUS, ZOROASTER, LAO TSE, BUDDHA....

Their words, their wisdom, can be like guides for our decisions, for our actions. If we question what to do or how to act in a situation, reflect back on the understanding expressed through these various teachers.

For myself, I find the teacher I turn to is JESUS. When I find myself perplexed, caught up in frustration or anger, I stop for a moment and ask myself " What would JESUS do in a situation like this?"

The answer comes instantly. He would forgive the intrusion, he would give love, and then he would continue on his way. Try it. What have you got to lose? Only your anger, frustration, and disappointments. And you have got so much to gain.

There is a technique I use, and one that works every time when I am confronted by a negative situation.

Let us say someone comes up to you in a state of anger, wanting to put you down, reject you, or insult you. First thing to do is to look directly into their eyes. The eyes are the windows to the soul. Then, evoke the eleventh commandment, the one that affirms: "Keep Thy Mouth Shut!". Third, in your consciousness say to that person silently, without moving your lips: "I love you."

Within five minutes of working this technique, and applying it sincerely, you are likely to find the other person dumfounded. It is as if he does not know what hit him. Either he may apologize for his action, or he may just walk away.

Let me share an incident I experienced in this regard. It was many years ago, during the early days of my career as a radio broadcaster. I was heading to work one hot Friday afternoon in August. It was about 3:30, and I was leaving Manhattan for Long Island by the 59th Street Bridge. I was feeling on top of the world at the time. I really enjoyed my work, and I liked my Job. I had just gotten a new car at the time. I was feeling really good about myself.

Of course, bliss without awareness gets back to the old ignorance bit. And so I was at the time. For while I was feeling great about myself and my own personal world, I had lost awareness of what was going on around me that Friday afternoon on the bridge.

Leaving New York on a Friday afternoon in August for Long Island is like joining an exodus of lemmings racing for the shore. The traffic was heavy, the situation complicated by ongoing construction on the bridge. Due to the construction and merging lanes, traffic narrowed down to a feeder lane to the upper level of the bridge.

Because of my happy state without awareness, I did not notice all the pent up anger and frustration around me that the other drivers were feeling.

So I was driving along, moving toward the narrowing of the roadway. Usually, cars will alternate in a merging situation. However, several taxi cabs in their race to nowhere pushed ahead of me. In all, I let three cabs go ahead of me. A fourth one came up,trying to push ahead of me. We were side by side, heading up the narrowing roadway.

I decided not to let him in ahead of me, and he was just determined to do so. We were inching along side by side as the roadway continued to narrow. I could see the cabdriver was very agitated. There was a farce in his back seat.

I smiled at the cabdriver. He responded by showing me his index finger. I smiled back at him. In turn, he screamed at me very loudly some profanity about my mother. I looked back over at him. I could see his face was livid with rage. He was clutching the steering wheel as though he was strangling someone. The fare in the back seat was freaking out by what was going on.

My eyes and the cabdriver's met once again as I was about to take my turn at the merge. I looked at the cabdriver, smiled, and mouthed the words: "I love you."

His reaction was completely insane. Whether he thought I was homosexual or what, he went totally out of control. He drove his cab forward, refusing to yield the right of way. Instead, he was driving his cab for about fifty yards along the metal divider, and as his cab scraped the metal barrier, sparks were flying.

It would have been simple for him to have turned the wheel to the right and disengaged his cab from the barrier. But he was in such a rage that not only did it blind his thinking, but his entire equilibrium.

This would not be much of a story, if there was not a follow-up. After we had gotten off the bridge, several miles down the highway, the cabdriver and I happened to pass again. But this time, when we passed each other, the most extraordinary thing happened. Instead of swearing and cursing at me, he was waving and laughing. For at least a moment, the power of love had transformed him.

Try something like this. It works. Say nothing, just let the power of love be felt. Can you? Can you forgive and give love?

Our relationships show a paradox. It is a paradox similar to the old chicken-egg controversy: what came first, the chicken or the egg? The same thing can be said of relationships. And that is: HOW CAN YOU LOVE ANOTHER IF YOU CANNOT LOVE YOURSELF. You can't. Not really. Not in the sense of love. That's why it is so important to become aware of ourselves. That is why it is essential to appreciate our qualities and respect our character. However, this does not mean we should give license to the self-aggrandizement of the ego personality, where people try to convince themselves and others, often through conspicuous consumption, that not only are they "good" people, but that they are "better people."

Such an attitude is not grounded in love for one's self. Rather, it is an attitude fostered and festered by the sense of insecurity, by a discord and disharmony within the self. And it is an attitude born of ignorance, a lack of understanding and awareness. So much for the ignorance is bliss bit.

However, by growing in awareness, you provide fertile ground for the true development of the self to be realized. As you start to see divinity in material manifestations (recognize the spirit in matter), you will begin to understand the truth to the affirmation that man is made in the image of GOD. With that increased understanding, you will be better able to love yourself. Love yourself not in the sense of the mortal ego personality but rather as a child of GOD, the striving spirit of the eternal soul.

When you can truly love yourself, then you can truly love another....

How often have you heard people say to one another: "love you?"—Despite what we might presume, this phrase is incredibly hollow. There is no substance to it, because it is impersonal by the lack of the "I". Without the "I" there is no commitment in the statement. Only a shallow expression.

63

I LOVE YOU. These are powerful words, for with the "I" we honestly express ourselves, our feelings and our commitment.

Many people fear these words, however. And why? Because they are afraid to commit themselves,in case commitment becomes attachment and obligation. It does not have to. For our primary commitment is in the evolution of ourselves. And relationships provide us the ground for self-mastery through relatedness.

LOVE is the most powerful force in the Universe. And when we see how effective the expression of love (unconditional love) is, we surely realize its phenomenal powers of transformation. There is one story I would like to share with you that illustrates this power.

As a healer, I find many people come through my door. There are many wounded souls in the world today. Some seeking help, sometimes in desperation, come to me for healing. One such person was Janet.

Janet was desperate when she came to me, for her physical body had become cancerous. The medical doctors she had seen had given her six months to live. This six months death sentence might be commuted, the doctors told her, if she would undergo an extensive operation to remove the rapidly spreading malignant growth on her left side. After the operation, the follow-up would be a regimen of chemotherapy and radiation treatments.

Janet was in total panic. She was touching base with that very fundamental issue of personal survival, and she was terrified of death. If she went into the hospital for the operation, she believed she would never come out alive. The medical doctors she saw were not supportive. The outlook was bleak. She went to various medical doctors, hoping their diagnosis would be different. But each of them predicted the same result.

Although at her wits end, Janet was determined to find an alternate way of treating her problem. She investigated the various options open to her, and decided upon healing. She had heard about my method of healing, SPIRITUAL HEALING. Believing she had nothing to lose, she gave herself permission to try it. After all, she rationalized, if healing did not work, then she would accept her medical doctors advice and submit to the operation and chemotherapy treatments.

Guided by her own personal instincts, Janet called me and set up an appointment. Whenever I meet a client, I first make it crystal clear that I can promise nothing, that I guarantee nothing. As a healer, I am only a channel for energy that flows from GOD. I am not the one who heals. It is he, the patient, who is the healer and the physician. Secondly, I *never* suggest that he should stop his medical treatment, no matter what it is. For that is not my decision to make, it is the patient's. After all, it is his life.

And in his life, he is the outward reflection of his inner condition. Therefore, when Janet came to me, I understood that Janet herself was the mental architect for the basic foundation, structure and creation of her disease (dis-ease). Janet was the cause of the cancer manifesting in her physical body.

This is not to imply that all cancer is created or manifested by psychological rules. All of us have cancer cells within our bodies, and all of us have the ability to manifest a latent condition into reality. However, my point here is to share with you a certain type of the cancer personality. Like music, one of but many variations. By casting light on our attraction of the possibility of cancer, we can lift ourselves above the causation, and become aware of the psychological traps from our conditioning environment.

When I met with Janet, she expressed the sense that her whole life was deteriorating. She had been dealt a cruel hand. She believed GOD was punishing her. Instead of looking within herself, she blamed everyone and everything around her for her problems.

She explained how her problem had started. It all began when her husband of 27 years ran off with another woman. Not that she presumed their life together was paradise. On the contrary, she told me that their relationship was an uneasy one. Their life together had not been all that loving. Both made demands on the other.

The day her husband ran off, he told her that he wanted out,

65

that he did not love her, that he was tired of his existence with her, and that he was in love with another woman.

Janet exploded. Emotionally, her security was shattered. Her whole life was about to end. Despite the conflicts and the lack of love between the two of them, she had learned to live with the nagging emotional pain. Perhaps she was dissatisfied, but she was content to live with the situation.

So when her husband confronted her with his feelings, when he told her of his intent, and when he packed his bags and left, Janet locked herself into a mental closet. Day after day, her thoughts were angry, hateful and filled with tremendous jealousy.

All of these damaging, negative thoughts collectively triggered a massive biochemical change within Janet's emotional—physical system. The shock to her bio-computer in the brain reached a dangerous level. And her adrenaline released into her body a psychological awareness of discomfort, sensations of heavy depression and the fright of being alone. The awful moments of disorientation, the bodily rushes of anxiety which she experienced increased her body tension and created a violent collision with the immune system. Janet became a living wreck.

Every day, when she returned to her apartment, the breeding ground of her discontent, she would review her life over and over again. She replayed all the old tapes. For in the apartment was her husband's picture, his favorite chair, his books, the walls he had painted. The reflection of his presence was everywhere in the apartment. And in that environment, Janet would sit down and feed hostile, negative thoughts to a negative situation.

As they do, all the negative thoughts she sent out came back to her tenfold. But she want not aware of this. Instead, she would send out hateful, jealous thoughts. She blamed the other woman for taking away her husband. No matter that their life together was less than conjugal bliss. Every waking moment, Janet projected hate and anger. She was in a state of emotional turmoil. She was feeding a negative situation negative energy.

Things started to happen. Janet lost her job. Friends stopped calling her. The walls of the apartment seemed to be closing in on her. She developed a pain in her left side. As the weeks went by, the pain became steadily worse. She sensed something was growing inside of her. The pain continued to worsen. Finally, in fear, she consulted her doctors. And they gave her the news. She had cancer, and six months to live.

When she came to me, I remember how heavy with depression she was. It looked like she was trying to crawl back inside herself. We talked. We talked about her life. About her marriage, about her likes and dislikes. All the while, she sat very rigid, listening, hoping that her prayers would be answered.

From her personal experiences in life, we moved to a discussion of life itself. I began telling her why we are here on this planet, and why things happen to us. We talked about how every life was different, and how each of us experiences different events for the varied lessons to be learned. I mentioned that when something has outlived its usefulness in our lives, it is taken from us. In our personal interactions, relationships are taken from us by death, divorce, rejection. Any of these creates a very painful experience. In personal relationships, you cannot have an experience solely by yourself. Both partners share, extracting differing experiences.

At this time in her life, Janet was going through a very profound experience. She was filled with two very destructive emotions. HATE AND ANGER, which were eating her alive, and the causation of her cancer.

Janet and I talked about life as being like a classroom. We go into a new grade, take on the conditions of that grade, the conditions of our environment, the conditions of the collective, and our classmates. If we pass the test, we graduate. We go on summer vacation.

As we talked about what we have learned, what we have yet to learn, it became apparent that Janet was a fast learner. She understood the philosophical concepts about reincarnation, about cause and effect, about karma,and lessons to be learned.

We discussed love, the true love, UNCONDITIONAL LOVE. We spoke about FORGIVENESS. From the abstract, we went back to her situation, her own personal condition.

I suggested to her that she could end her suffering if she so desired.

How, she asked, determined to put an end to her pain.

I told her that first she should put away all images of her husband. All things that belonged to him, all traces of him. That included removing his books, his favorite chair, his pictures. By so doing, she would put into action the riddance for herself of reflective memory. I mentioned she should change her apartment, by rearranging the furniture, repainting the walls and redecorating her environment. This was the first step in loosening the hold of the disquieting thoughts and negative emotions.

Janet did these things. She cleaned out almost everything that had belonged to her previous life, to her life with her husband. She redecorated the entire apartment. As she did so, her outlook on life started to change, for the better. She had a sense that may be this process was actually going to work. Her consciousness started to shift, a positive feeling taking the place of the negative emotions she had floundered in.

With that shift in consciousness, Janet also began to realize that the other woman had nothing to do with taking her husband away. And she recognized that she could no longer blame the other woman for her cancer. Be releasing the hold of the negative emotions upon her, she found she could forgive the other woman.

When she called me, she mentioned the cancer had stopped hurting. She said she hardly felt any pain at all.

On Janet's next visit, we spoke again about love, unconditional love. Her belief was becoming stronger, and she was now ready for the big test. Could she work out the remaining psychological blocks, the resistance to letting go, of completely surrendering and embracing the unconditional to someone *she thought she loved?*

With the recognition that the other woman was not responsible for taking her husband away, she began to send LOVE to the other woman. At first, she had resistance, for the negative emotions and destructive thoughts were battling for their survival. But the moment she could send that woman love in total honesty, she experienced a strange fluttering in her side.

Weeks before, the cancer had stopped hurting. Now, to her very great surprise, she sensed that not only had the cancer stopped growing and spreading, but that it was actually shrinking. It was a bizarre feeling for her, as if someone had let the air out of a balloon.

Yet, as this phenomena occurred, she realized that LOVE, unconditional love, was healing her cancer, healing herself.

Janet progressed in her consciousness. Not only was she able to forgive and send love to the other woman, she was also able to get beyond the pain and hurt she felt from her husband's actions. Instead, she projected love and forgiveness to her husband, expecting nothing in return, but honestly feeling that she could rejoice in his new success.

Weeks later, she reported that her cancer was gone. Not just shrinking, but gone, completely. When she went back for a visit with her medical doctor, he was astounded. Whereas before, when he had pronounced a death sentence on her, this time he gave her a clean bill of health. The cancer was gone.

Janet's case in but one example of many where the power of forgiveness and love can turn our lives around, even when it seems that there may be no hope, no possibility.

To follow up on Janet's life conditions, her whole life has changed for the better. She realized that her neediness had emotionally created her problems. And with that awareness, the self-revelation, her life became brighter. People started to call her again. She was offered a new job. She became involved in another relationship and married the man. They moved to upstate New York. She had made her peace with her first husband, who had married the other woman and moved to California. And she and her first husband are nowgood friends.

For me, to be part of the process, as a channel for the healing, is a glory and a blessing. It always serves to reinforce and reconfirm my admiration for the master JESUS. For JESUS was truly one of the greatest healers to walk this earth. We have heard of his miracles, of his abilities to heal.

Never did JESUS see a person as deformed. He always saw them whole, in divine perfection, as his FATHER has created them.... PERFECT.

To JESUS, there was only imperfect thought. With his mind enveloped in the CHRIST consciousness, he was aware of the causation for *any* physical infirmities. By visualizing a person as he knew he was, perfect, made in the image of the FATHER—that energy created a wholeness and the imperfection in that person vanished.

Just as Janet's faith in LOVE healed her, so too will your own personal faith heal you. You are the one who must do it. It won't be done for you. You must put your faith into action. Two of the precepts of faith in action are FORGIVENESS and UNCONDITIONAL LOVE. Forgiveness erases causation.

No one said it would be easy. Neither does it have to be that hard. The more you practice, like a muscle toned by use, the more you will be able to put your faith in action. As you do, your perception will become clearer. You will be able to see the process and your causation in life conditions, in the way Janet and I walked through her reflections, going from the symptoms back to the causation. By touching base with the reasons behind her taking on cancer, we could correct the emotions and psychic implant from that causal event. Just as Janet released herself from the hold of negative emotions and truly healed herself, you can do the same.

Dependency and possessiveness are concurrent curses in our relationships. They are major lessons we all have to learn in relatedness.

One of the areas of relatedness that is especially difficult, because it is so subtle and therefore potentially deceptive, is family. Many of our relationships are by choice—- our marriage partner, our business partner, our friends. And we can choose to end those relationships. Although it may not always be easy to extricate ourselves from the relationships by choice, we can still do so. But with family....

They say blood is thicker than water. So is quicksand.

FAMILY relationships can be especially difficult because they are born from dependency. If they are parent-child relationships, that is especially true. For the child was dependent upon his parents while he was a baby. And often parents become dependent upon their children in their later years. This dependency is also part of the early conditioning within the family structure: parent-child, sibling-sibling, parent-sibling.

All sorts of rivalries may be allowed within defined parameters, but a strong sense of obligation is also built-in to family relations. By that early conditioning, we are taught to accept from someone within the family what we might never accept from someone in a relationship of choice. And why? "Because it is family."

In the name of family, we often meet some of our greatest tests. One of mine came through my brother. As a child, I looked up to my older brother. I wanted to be like him, even to the point of following him and enlisting in the NAVY when I was nearly of age.

After serving his enlistment time in the Navy, my brother reenlisted in the Marine Corps. During World War II, he traveled the world. He became a dedicated career man, the epitome of the "esprit de corps" associated with that branch of the Armed Services. When the war ended, my brother reenlisted. He came back to the States and became a D. I. (drill instructor) at various marine training camps.

His career was unfolding. He received a number of merit commendations. Not only was his career flourishing, his personal life was also opening up. Between World War II and the Korean conflict, he got married and started a family. He had a son and a daughter. During this period, I did not have a lot of contact with him. I was married at the time, and had my own life to contend with. But he was my brother, and I was still very proud of him.

When the Korean War broke out, my brother was sent into combat. Secretly, he always likes to have a cause to work for and through. And this was it. He saw a lot of action in Korea, as did of

71

his comrades, and was himself wounded by shrapnel in his legs. He received the Purple Heart and other awards.

Combat was a way of life for my brother. He had but one thought: The duty of the military. Kill or be killed. Therefore, when the Korean war ended and he left the service briefly, he was like a fish out of water. The massive nervous tensions that had been within him, tensions he was able to release through combat duty, increased without an outlet.

He and his family moved all around the country. His family wanted roots, a stable life. He wanted adventure. My brother became frustrated and started to drink more and more. He reentered the service. He was a master sergeant in the Marine Corps when the Vietnam involvement began. He was sent into action. His main love was fulfilled. For a time the combat within himself was relieved by the physical combat in war. That war ended for him as well.

He came back to the States. He was lean, tanned and eager. He had made it through that Southeast Asian hell. He had survived. On his return, my brother was stationed at Parris Island, South Carolina, where he trained recruits. This lasted for a while, until he lost interest. He left the service, with a chest full of ribbons. He was ready for the world. But was the world ready for him? He believed that all doors would open to a veteran who had served his country.

It did not happen that way. My brother became frustrated, confused. He and his wife were constantly arguing. As days became weeks, then months, with no opportunities opening up to him, my brother sank lower and lower into the turmoil of his own inner world. His insecurities, his fears, his frustrations started to eat at him. The combat was engaged, the war within himself.

One of the greatest travesties of the Armed Services, especially for those who have seen combat, is the lack of deprogramming from service life when the veteran re-enters civilian life. We have seen it depicted in the post-traumatic syndromes of many recent veterans, who are unable to cope, and to move beyond that experience of hell. So it was for my brother.

After many years in combat, he just did not know how to live in a non-combat situation. He had never been debriefed, de-programmed, readjusted. Combat increased in his home life: The arguments with his wife, his inability to deal effectively with his children. Questions of what he could do for a living gnawed at him. The doors of opportunity had not opened. His potential employment picture was reduced to being a security guard, or a cop in a small town. Maybe an insurance salesman, or any kind of salesman. He did not know. What he did know was that the possibilities contrasted starkly with his combat image, the fantasies of self-aggrandizement, the delusions of grandeur.

Inertia ensued. My brother was unable to move on. He was in a paralytic state of STOP ... NO-GO. His wife divorced him. He started to drink again. The more he drank, the more negative he became. He began to lie and cheat. He lost every job he tried. He became addicted to the bottle. Unconsciously, our mother supported his habit. He would ask her for money, telling her he needed the funds to travel for a job. In truth, the money was paying for his drinking habit. He started to steal.

My brother traveled around, and tapped into our mother's friends. He would go to their houses and knock on their doors. He would say he had a truck full of antiques broken down on the highway, and could they lend him money to make the necessary repairs. He would tell them he would mail them a check.

This went on for a period of time. He sank deeper into the booze. He found himself down in the Bowery in New York City, a bum, reliving his past from the bottom of a bottle.

One cold winter day, when it was sleeting outside, there was a knock at my door. I opened the door. to see my brother in shirt sleeves, soaking wet, and filthy dirty. He smelled of booze, urine and waste. It shook me to my core to see my brother like that.

Remember, this was the brother I looked up to, revered, and wanted to be like when I was a child. But he was not there. Before me stood a man who had given into his fears, weaknesses and insecurities. He begged to come in. I was angry with him for using our mother to feed his addiction. But at that moment I could not make a judgement. He was cold and hungry, he begged to come in. He was crying. I barred the entrance with my body. I told him he could not enter. I told him to straighten himself out, and turn himself in. And then I slammed the door in his face.—On my brother.

I screamed inside myself with pain and rage that I should have to do this...to my brother. The brother I loved. I sat and cried for hours. I pleaded with GOD, praying that I had done the right thing.

Immediately, I was plagued by guilt and fear that something would happen to my brother on account of my actions. I RISKED the fear of his death, to do the thing I thought right. I knew that Alcoholics Anonymous insists you close the door on a loved one's face. For they believe the shock may help bring the alcoholic loved one to some semblance of normalcy, and the desire to get himself straight. I knew all this, because I had counseled others for their own personal problems, for their own loved ones. But this was my brother, and the test was for me, not another.

My brother did turn himself in. He sought help at Serenity House in Connecticut. He left many times, but he always returned. He realized he needed help. It takes massive courage to work through the turmoil of personal conflict. My brother made it.

Today, my brother has his life together. He is married again and has a good relationship with his children. He has grown tremendously, his consciousness expanding, and he is still growing.

What an experience that man put himself through. What pain. And yet, the lessons he learned have contributed to his ever-expanding consciousness. He is my brother, and I love him.

Can you? Can you love your brother, your sister, a stranger on the street? CAN YOU LOVE?

Indeed, you can love. And I mean truly love, without the conditions, without the expectations. You can do it. You probably have done so in the past.

Remember when you "fell" in love? Perhaps the other person

seemed to come from out of nowhere. But he appeared in your life. And you loved him with all of your heart and soul. If you have experienced such relatedness, you can well appreciate the power of the love force. For when you are in love, you feel as though you could conquer the world. No task is beyond your reach. Why? Because you are energized. You are in rapport with life itself. And as a result, you become more creative, more vital, more joyful. Life takes on a golden hue for you.

Does it still? It can, you know.

Community

Man lives in groups. He joins together into communities. We have all heard the saying that no man is an island unto himself. We live in interaction with others. We live in society.

What is society? Basically, society is the living materialized thought form of the collective consciousness. Society *reflects* the state of mankind. Together, you and I and all the others in our community create the patterns and standards of our society. And as such, society is not static, but rather in constant flux in accord with our thought processes and our actions.

Look at society today and you see the state of mankind.

Although each of us is here to evolve ourselves, to grow and develop beyond our present capabilities, we do so within the parameters of relationships and community. However, just as we discussed in self-mastery through relatedness, we should recognize that society has effects upon our self-mastery as well.

In society, we see the power of group dynamics in operation. Conditioning by peer pressure often leads to a blind acceptance of the conventions and standards of society. We assume it is easier to go along. The line of least resistance. Of course, by doing so we may be stunting our own growth and evolution.

It is not easy to swim against the current. Especially in our day and age. The reinforcement of the collective consciousness is not only experienced by our own personal interaction with the world. In this era of the communications revolution, the mass consciousness is being broadcast twenty-four hours every day out onto the air waves on all forms of energy frequencies. To be in this world but not of it is a difficult task. In our present time, it seems harder because of the constant bombardment of the collective psyche's thought forms, magnified and enhanced by global communications systems.

Turn on your television any time. That wizard's wonder of magic and imagination has been reduced to a glorification of immediate ego gratification. Although gross characterizations, so many of our television programs revolve around the following emotions: Greed, fear, lust, anger, hate, violence. How many television programs concentrate on, even to the point of extolling, the negative emotions?

Where are the programs of faith and uplifting, the shows that entertain and enlighten? There are some, only a few. The television industry programs largely to the negative emotions. And the consequence? A reinforcement of the negative in the collective consciousness upon each individual viewer and, on occasion, with dire results. We have probably all heard or read about some of the tragedies that have followed certain television showings. With the power of suggestion enforced by thousands of minds focussing upon that dramatized action on the television screen, individuals have acted out the bizarre behavior they have seen on television. In our legal system now, the debate rages over the question whether a temporary insanity defense can be claimed due to the influence of a television program.

When we, as individuals, get to the point of realizing that the negative emotions of the collective consciousness are only a hindrance to our own self growth and development, that is a time of critical choice, It is a crossroads in our lives. For it is a time when we not only question society's attitudes, but also wonder whether those attitudes are in harmony with our own internal feelings, that growing sense of true individual expression within ourselves.

At that time of critical choice, many people decide not to go forward. There is too much resistance. It is too radical to change. Instead, these people opt for the ways and mores of the herd consciousness, once again. They figure it is easier to go along. It may appear to be, but in the long run it is not.

That sense of growing individuality within you may be buried effectively, but it can never be snuffed out. There will be another time, another crossroad.

For those who decide to go against the grain, it is not easy. It demands all the fortitude and will power of a true gladiator, off to do battle with the dragons of societal conditioning ingrained in your consciousness. It takes great courage to stand up for your convictions when they contrast so fundamentally with society's notions. It takes great stamina. You may be ridiculed, you may be alienated. Why? Because you have become a threat, a threat to the herd consciousness.

Part of the herd consciousness is getting while the getting is good. Born from individuals' lack of self-awareness, society reflects our individual attempts to hoard, accumulate and get as much for ourselves as we can in as short a period of time. It is known as maximum return.

In optimizing potential for maximum return, society tends to cut corners. Morality gives way to amorality, and then immorality. Aberrant behavior becomes justified because everybody does it, and if you do not, then you are just plain stupid.

In maximizing return, there is often the tendency on the part of society to focus solely on the immediate effect and to ignore or neglect the long-range consequences. We see it today, where societies have abused their resources, laid waste to their environments. All in the name of forward progress. Some progress!

We are takers, not givers. We have lost the balance in life. The North American Indian talks of man being the guardian of the earth, as being the caretaker.

That wisdom has gone unappreciated. As the white man settled west across the North American continent, Indians were herded into reservations. The white man celebrated his victory in gaining the land the Indians had lost. However, what the white man never understood, and still does not understand, is that man cannot own the land. He is here to take care of it.

Some caretakers we have become. We have taken from the

earth, without giving back in return. Except our toxic wastes, our decimation of the countryside. And the consequences?

Mankind is at a crossroad. He has poisoned his waters, polluted his skies. He has turned a paradise on earth to a noxious wasteland. Instead of being in rapport with life's natural cycles and the abundance given to us on this earth, we have pillaged and raped our home, our planet earth.

With our consciousness based upon fear and a unrelieved greed, we have created for ourself: LACK. Many of our brothers and sisters are hungry, millions dying from famine. We are quickly diminishing our fresh water resources. We have created for ourselves all the problems derived from our misguided actions.

If we continue in this same vein, the outcome seems inevitable. The end is near. Or is it?

Inevitability smacks of an inability to change. Man has the opportunity to change at any point. Certainly, the problems won't immediately go away. We have reaped from what we have sown. But we can find solutions.

You may disagree. You may seem to feel that the factors impacting societal conditions today are overwhelming, beyond corrective action. They are not.

It is only a question of man changing his consciousness, altering his perspective. And how will society effect this? First of you, BY YOU, BY ME.

By changing gears in your outlook, by your own growth made stronger by having to go against conventional opinion, you and I, and the others who are devoted to the unfolding of our spirit while in matter will indeed have an impact.

Like the pebble dropped into a pond, our every action has a rippling effect, the reach of which we cannot fully appreciate, or perhaps presently understand. No matter. What is important is your faith, and implementing that faith into action, by realizing your spirit in matter, and manifesting your spirit in action.

It is not easy. Nobody said it would be. Or if they did, they were not telling the truth.

Part of the collective consciousness in society is the accepted belief and attitude. One of the cornerstones of this belief is religion. Not the kernel of truth that each religious teaching has as its foundation. Rather, religion as a structured orthodoxy, as an institution of prescribed rights and wrongs.

Many people assume that by growing spiritually, you become more religious. Not so. Unfortunately, in our day and age religion no longer truly ministers to the human spirit, nor truly comforts the human soul. Today, religion has become an institution, seeking to increase its financial position and spread its political power base. We see religion now ever more involved in the secular world, in temporal existence, turning its back on its real purpose of providing guideposts to the spirit along the way.

Just think how religion has been used in the past. It has done much to blind the individual's growth, to thwart the unfolding of true individual creative expression. Instead, it reinforces the collective consciousness to the detriment of the self-developing individual.

How has religion done this? By emphasizing our fears, our guilt, our sense of unworthiness and separation. Religion holds out carrots with the threat of sticks, but the promised carrot is an elusive quest that religion holds out beyond our present reach.

How many religions concern themselves with the future? With the salvation coming not now, not in the present, but in some hereafter. It is often necessary for religion to promulgate future salvation, for it provides the dependency needed for the continued faith of its adherents. Otherwise, today's religions would serve no purpose. They would not have the hold they do, keeping so many of us captive to our fears and guilt.

We will talk later about true religious teachings. For the moment, however, consider what I have said. What buttons have I pressed? Are you silently fuming from the words you have just read? Are you angrily swearing epithets at me for some imagined sacrilege? Or can you see the truth to what I say?

Our journey through life is entangled by temptations and tests that are ever so subtle. Sometimes, we get lost. That is OK. It is all part of our progress.

I mentioned religion in this context for you to consider how even the most apparently safe and nurturing shelters may not always be safe harbors in a friendly port.

There is a saying that life does not get easier, it gets clearer. That clarity of mind, clarity of purpose, comes to us through our increased awareness. The more aware we become, the subtler the tests. It is all part of the process of honing ourselves so that like a diamond we can reflect the true light through our being flawlessly.

While fear has been used to win our belief in various religious systems, or more to the fact, religious organizations, its converse emotion has been just as effective in societal conditioning. GREED has been one of the strongest motivating influences for the lives of many fellow travelers.

A FOCUS ON LACK GENERATES FEAR. TO COMPENSATE FOR FEAR, WE REACT WITH GREED. The bull and the bear of economic conditions. Roots nourished by our sense of our individual selves: a lack, something missing, within ourselves.

The very first questioning of real purpose or meaning in a individual's life begins the slow, often cumbersome, journey, a path fraught with dragons and lairs along the way. We stand four-square against conventional opinion, the accepted knowledge. It is like spitting into the wind.

But what's interesting is that no matter how strong the resistance, the growing individual will also sense an increase in resilience, a developing inner strength born from a growing peace in pursuing the quest of self-discovery and enlightenment.

We Never Get More Than We Can Handle

Believe it! You may not want to, but you will have to give that one up too. For to think otherwise sets you up for defeat before you even begin. It is a real limitation, a real blockage tied to an acceptance of present security, no matter how grim the conditions, because of the unwillingness to "risk" change.

And what's the alternative? In our society, running on empty, a lack of true self-respect and awareness, creates constant caroming between those two heavies: Fear and greed.

Those two cornerstones to our HELL ON EARTH. How many of us have imagined what it would be like to be financially wealthy? We imagine how all our problems would be solved. We would be on easy street. Of course, it is a beautiful fantasy, but unfortunately one that is out of sync with reality. People with money have no fewer problems than those without. The problems are different. The fears do not go away. Sometimes people are driven to acquire great wealth by their sense of lack. They believe, as we are led to believe by our image makers, that by gaining vast amounts of money they will relieve their fear, their sense of lack.

It does not always work that way. For some people are driven to accumulate vast sums of money, then fear that what they have been able to hoard will somehow be taken from them. In reaction, they bury it. In bank vaults, in interest-bearing bonds, in some avenue to maintain, perhaps even safely increase their worth.

Material worth, that is. But often, these very same people are those who live in poverty. Maybe not a material poverty, but certainly a spiritual poverty. All that they have accumulated, all that they have gained, is like some hollow victory, the taste of like bitter ashes.

Everything in life is in a state of motion, constant movement

To gain material goods and then to hoard them from a sense of fear is not in sync with the material function of recycling. Think about it. Think about it in terms of the natural, virtually automatic, function we perform.

In breathing, we breathe in and we breathe out. If we do not we die. In nourishing our bodies, we ingest food. But we also perform the natural function of eliminating the wastes from our food intake. If we do not, we get constipated. And we become sick.

So too with money. For money is energy, green energy if you will. If we keep that energy in a state of inertia by hoarding it, we too become ill.

Money creates a false sense of power. If man does not know how to handle money, it will destroy him.

How many examples are there of those who have suddenly gained great wealth only to have it make them much worse off than they were before? In recent years, with the increasing popularity of lotteries and get-rich-quick schemes, we have seen the examples repeated over and over. There is a saying that money is the root of all evil. I disagree. The problem is not with the green energy, but rather man's use or, more appropriately, misuse of that energy.

One arena in which this becomes chillingly evident is when a man of wealth is nearing his death. Since he cannot take it with him when he goes, a greediness suddenly; erupts among the man's relatives and close associates. It is not rare to see people of good character and quality transformed into scheming, conniving types, who plan and plot how they will get a share of the money.

The intrigues in families that occur regarding legacies and inheritances are mind-boggling. It can made people sick. For a schizophrenic depression is likely to occur. The schizophrenia being between a real LOVE for the one who is nearing death and a total GREED for their money. Some bounty, some reward.

The LOVE for money, the total concentration on material accumulation, eventually leads to devastation. To repeat, money is not bad. It is energy. How we use that energy, how we make use of money, is the determining factor whether it is good or bad. If you have money, keep it in the flow.

Remember, whatever you give out comes back to you tenfold.

There are so many things to learn. So many things to re-learn. And the time to re-learn them is now. For the twentieth century is a period filled with enormous change to both man and his home, the planet earth. With these changes come great testings indeed.

Never before has man's scientific knowledge and technological advances catapulted mankind to the brink of self-annihilation. Certainly, our understandings and discoveries have been remarkable. We have the ability to split the atom, to get beneath matter into sub-atomic forces. But what have we done with this knowledge? We have created missiles and weapons, to the extent that we can now blow our earth apart many times over. From fear, from our own sense of lack, we have used our knowledge not for the betterment of mankind, or for the improvement of quality of life on earth. Rather, our recent discoveries have become for us like a Pandora's box, unleashing destructive capabilities and the potential for man's extinction.

But why?

Because we have drawn upon our rational, reasoning mind, a state of consciousness focused solely on matter. Because we have negated the intuitive, higher mind, we have lost sight of spiritual and social sciences. This imbalanced state of mind in the collective consciousness is the cause for the turmoil and chaos to come.

The handwriting is already on the wall. We see it in the graffiti scrawled imperiously on public buildings, sacred monuments, beautiful edifices. Take a ride on a New York City subway train. Almost every car is marred by the graffiti of someone seeking to leave their mark, by crying out their individuality. It is often a pathetic display, but one that is part of the natural evolution.

For we have reached a state of overpopulation. The collective consciousness has fallen out of sync with the natural process of procreation. Today, we breed with no thought regarding outcome. Instead of creating a child from love, children are brought forth from our mere animal instinct of having sex. And so, a child is born. A child that may not truly be wanted, or respected for his own personality, his own evolution.

What's likely to occur is that the child has no way of expressing itself within the family structure, a structure that in our day and age is increasingly deteriorating. With no outlet for creative self-expression, with no respect from parental figures, the young soul goes forth and scratches his name, logo, or sentiments across public walls.

History has a way of repeating itself. Until the lessons are learned, society will go through similar patterns in its cycles. One of the most obvious, of course, is the pattern of war and peace. It is as though because man has not found real peace within himself, he cannot live peacefully with his neighbors. War breaks out, and the emotions of heat and negativity spend themselves. Peace then follows, with a blind hope that the previous war was the one to end all wars.

Until the next one. And so it goes. But is it inevitable for man, for society, to be in constant conflict? No. It does not have to be that way.

Certainly, there are similar cycles, and similar phases within those cycles. But mankind's response to social cycles can spell the difference between aggression through war and a catalyst to transform the collective consciousness. In the past, mankind has chosen war. What will mankind do in the future?

That decision, that choice, resides within each one of us. For we are society, by our individual examples and deeds we can truly effect great changes within the collective.

After all, change is a continual part of the process. And conscious change allows for a realignment in sync with nature, with natural law. We will discuss some of these natural laws subsequently. And we will also give techniques by which each of us can better our own lives and thereby serve as catalysts for the changes in the life of the collective.

While it may not be easy to go against the collective consciousness, it is indeed a natural part of an individual's evolution. For society's belief and attitudes regarding life and the living have fallen completely out of sync with true reality. Mankind has developed his lower mind, the computer mind with its wonderful capabilities. In so doing, however, mankind has locked himself into an experiential world filtered through the analytical, reasoning mind.

We think things through. But in our thinking process we rarely question the abstracts, or premises, behind our review and consideration of life experience. Because we are conditioned by society, we accept the underlying standards as being true. They are not.

In developing the lower mind, man separated himself from that intuitive link to the supra-consciousness, that connection with GOD and natural law. As in all cycles, so too with this one. In this century, man has rediscovered his higher mind. On an individual effort, people are starting to seek reconnection to that aspect of mind. There is a quiet yearning afoot, the natural yearning in an individual's self-development and awareness.

It is stronger during this period in man's evolution and provides the seeker with some solace in the swim against the tide of conventional wisdom. There will be times when we may err and lose our way. We too will fall into the traps and pitfalls of the collective patterns created by society. We will find ourselves doing things because of society's influence. The impact of group dynamics.

It is OK. It is all part of the process. It may be necessary to get sucked into societal patterns and pitfalls every now and then. To judge our actions as mistakes or errors is to condemn without full understanding. Besides, our potential liability to make transgressions through the power of the collective consciousness keeps us humble, and spiritual arrogance is an inevitable test along the path. Secondly, that very transgression increases our awareness, hones our vigilance along the quest.

And that quest? Our purpose? The realization of our selves and the true expression of our individual creativity through unconditional love.

By your actions, you will be known. And your example, your being, will impact society and influence the collective conditions.

Ridding ourselves of the programmed patterns inculcated by the limitations of societal conditioning is one of the tests in our self-development, in our growth. It may be difficult, but it is not impossible. It may seem that way, but it is not. You have to be able to believe in magic, in the power of change and transformation. Can you? Will you?

During this time in man's evolution when we are seeking to reconnect with the higher mind, all sorts of groups and philosophies have sprung up which promise to provide the means, often an easy way, to develop the higher mind.

If we are weak within ourselves, we are likely to be seduced by one group or one individual into believing that they can make it easier for us. They promise us the way, they provide answers to our questions, and offer us techniques by which we can speed our process of development.

Seeker Beware

The journey of growth and self-development is an arduous one, and often a lonely one. There are many seductions and temptations along the way. One of those is the false prophets that presently abound.

Like a carnival fun-house, groups and individuals today are barking their claims of being the one true answer, the one true teaching to lead you to Nirvana, down the glory road to paradise, heaven on earth. All you have to do is join. Some will say that they are sanctioned by the blessed Virgin Mary, or that GOD has chosen their group as the one to bring truth to the world.

Seeker be aware

Be aware of those who have rigid structures, wear uniforms or demand uniformity. These groups attract people. Some of those they attract are innocents, others emotional cripples who seek to escape their everyday life wanting a miracle to happen. For them, a miracle did happen they joined a group.

Although it may seem extreme to you, many of these present day groups have a certain similarity to the phenomenon that overtook the German nation in the 1930's. Hitler's Third Reich offered to fill a void in the German nation. We are aware of the consequences, but we have forgotten the lessons that were to be learned.

In these so-called "spiritual" groups today, many of our individual wants, what we believe to be our "needs", are fulfilled. Similar to Hitler's Third Reich, these present-day groups also fill a certain void, by offering us the temptations of filling our wants. And what are these wants? Among them are such emotions as:

Wanting to have a purpose or meaning in one's life. Many groups purport to be on a mission, and that mission is often the lofty one of saving the world. (How is that for spiritual arrogance?). It is effective, for who isn't tempted by bring a chosen one to bring truth, light and love to the world?

Wanting a relatedness with other people. Because the purpose of the group is shared by the individuals involved in the group, there is a common shared experience which allows for a mood of sharing one's self with others in the group. This attitude is fostered by the group, for it reinforces the individual commitment to the group. Consequently, in many groups, there is a certain permissiveness expressed between people. It may be given the name of free love, but often it is the sharing in sex, without the stigma of a one night stand.

Wanting our basic needs to be covered. Food, shelter, even a pittance of income are often provided by a group.

Wanting friends.

Wanting knowledge or understanding.

Wanting something to do.

Whatever the emotion we seek to fulfill, spiritual groups do indeed seek to fill that want, that sense of need.

Perhaps the strongest pull toward a group is that it allows us to give up responsibility for our own individual evolution. It is as if by joining a group, we can close the door on all the clutter in our own personal consciousness.

This is not to say that all groups are tarnished or disreputable. Nor does it deny the power of group dynamics that can afford a catalyst for the individual's growth.

But, please, realize that the majority of the inner work, that most of our individual readjustment, has to be done by us. As individuals, by our selves.

I am not saying you shouldn't joint a group, or shouldn't share in your experience with others. Not at all. What I am asking is that you be *aware* of the group with the fancy trappings, and the use of words that sound so heavenly.

Always investigate the group before you join. Do not be fooled or misled by sham appearance. Really look, before you leap. Do the leaders of the group live up to their teachings? Do they practice what they preach? Are they living their philosophy? Are they able to step down and meet you on a one to one basis? Or do they stay perched upon their throne?

In our century, millions are turning to the group experience. Community sharing is certainly good if it is kept to true brotherhood. But, unfortunately, in practice it is rarely the case. What tends to occur within groups are that petty jealousies begin to arise. There are those caught in self-aggrandizement who seek power within the group. The power elite confuses the message, adding to the friction, and eventually the group decays.

Some groups thrive on a strong disciplined fear, from their teacher or leader. With a ritual and dogma as structured as the U.S. Marines, these groups I call COSMIC BOOT CAMPS. They are children of the Third Reich. For they draw upon mythologist understanding of natural law, a mystique of technique and elaborate ritual to bend the individual will to the group force directed by the leader.

However, if that is what the individual needs to experience at this place in time, so be it. To the innocents, I say: SEEKER BEWARE.

There is a great deal of seduction among the groups. They will accost you on the street, on public transportation. They will use whatever means or manner to get you. At an airport, at a railway station, they may come up to you and thrust a book into your hand. They will tell you it is yours, free, a gift with no strings attached. Then they will ask you to donate in the CAUSE OF GOD. Of course, if you accept your free gift and happen to walk away without giving a donation, they are likely to go into a fit of hysteria.

I am not saying these followers of one teacher or another are malicious. On the contrary. Often, these souls are brain-washed individuals who truly believe they are doing the work of their master. They may be a nuisance, they may be intrusive. But they provide another gift. Another test.

That test, that gift, is to be able to realize that these followers feel you need the group experience. If you find a group that feels right to you, a group whose teachings and practices you have really investigated, then join. But be aware! Do not lose sight of the purpose in the group experience. And that purpose? To extract from that group, from it's teachings, what you need for your own growth, your own self-development.

Some people join groups for that reason, In fact, a majority do so. However, once inside the group experience, our reason for joining the group, our purpose within the group, becomes confused. We become tempted, seduced by what the group can provide us in filling our wants, satisfying our desires.

Instead of listening to the teacher within, that voice within ourselves that truly knows and understands, we listen instead to the leader of the group. We start to question the rightness of that small voice within ourselves. We assume our insights, our understandings, to be something less than those of the leader or teacher of the group. We forego the role of the active gladiator out to slay our own personal dragons along the quest to self-development. Instead, we become the follower, a passive participant to the force of the group.

Have total faith in the teacher who lies within

Because of our sense of personal lack, due to our desires to relate to others, we sometimes forget the teacher within each one of us. Or if we acknowledge its existence, we question its accuracy, its reliability. Don't.

Accept yourself where you are. See yourself for who you are. Still your mind and listen in silence, so that you can hear the teacher who is within you.

In our day and age, when we are constantly bombarded by all sorts of external stimuli, it is hard to quiet the mind and turn inward. It is also essential.

The power of the collective consciousness is stronger in our

90

present time by reason of the media. Societal attitudes and beliefs are reinforced by the power of the media. To a greater or lesser extent, each one of us has been programmed by the massive hypnotic influence of television. The majority of people are addicted to the television, especially in our United States. Are you aware that on a per capita basis, the television is on in our homes six hours of every day? One fourth of the entire day, about one third of our waking hours, are spent with the television going. Perhaps we use it as background noise. Perhaps we have it on as a companion when we are alone.

The influence of television, the programming it airs, reinforces the massive self-gratification we see today. No one really thinks for himself. He depends on others to tell him what to do. This tendency reinforces the appeal of the group experience.

There is a minority which is bucking the tide. There are people who seek to bring about change, to incorporate the spiritual concepts of enlightenment in their daily lives, and awaken the stirring consciousness. Are you one of them? Will you be one of us?

What is the alternative? To willingly go along, as the line of least resistance, with societal mores and actions. To become sucked up into the constant need of possessing more and more. This need is never sated, the thirst for acquisition never quenched. Except when we change our consciousness.

Water will always reach its own level. Like will always attract like. Whatever we worship, we receive. Both in our individual lives, and in the life of the collective.

Negativity breeds negativity. Think negative thoughts, and you create negative conditions. Be confused in your thinking, and you will create confusion in your environment.

The chaos and confusion in our world today had a starting point. It did not materialize out of nowhere. Rather, the starting point was born from a consciousness mired in negativity — fear, greed, a focus solely on material goods.

This negativity is reflected in all forms of media. Even where there is some claim for objectivity in reporting the facts—just the facts—the subjectivity in thinking intrudes.

Think about it. When you watch a news program on television, how often do you see a "good news" story? If there is one, it is often a human interest feature to which three minutes of coverage is given. Buried at the end of the news broadcast, compared to maximum broadcast time given to the "negative" news, these human interest features become lost in the shuffle.

What do we see on the news? All the things wrong in our society. We see people starving to death in Africa. We see others fighting to their death in Central America. We see terrorist activities causing death in the Middle East. We see the homeless, the destitute, the unemployed in our United States. We see budget crises, prices going up, an economy that rebounds from recession to expansion with the latent threat of a depression around the corner. We see the crime reports with the muggings, the killings, the rapings and kidnappings. We see all sorts of evidence of mankind moving into a self-destructive mode.

Is it any wonder that the nightly news tends to depress us? Is it any wonder that people who are fed this type of reality night after night, day in—day out, are frightened nearly to death? Not really.

Where the question, where the true wondering comes in, is why we attune ourselves to that kind of reality. Perhaps you may say that the awareness of society's plight is necessary in order for it to be corrected.

And I would agree with you. However, what I would question is whether we become aware of that reality? Or does that reality suck us into an attitude, a regimen, that is based upon fear?

Look around, and I believe you are likely to agree that too much concentration on the ills of the world can create ills within ourselves. People live in fear today.

Have you ever visited someone who lives in New York City? Ring their apartment doorbell, and you wait for the door to be opened. Much of your waiting is likely to be while the person inside unlocks the three or four locks he's got on his door.

Many of us have become prisoners within our own homes.

We fear to venture outside. We are afraid to go out into the world. And why? Because we have become programmed by our news media to all the fears and frights of living.

Some living, some life. Not only do we become afraid of life, but we take these fears and worries into our bodies, creating the conditions for dis-ease to gestate, for illness to appear.

Look at our society. For all the wonders of our technology, for all our scientific advances, how healthy are we? Perhaps we have eradicated malaria, smallpox, the bubonic plague. But our society is ravaged by other plagues—-the cancers that have reached epidemic proportions, the new viruses we know so little about, the self-limiting diseases of our society's sickness.

It does not have to be that way. You know it. Otherwise, you would not be reading through this book.

The eradication of the various illnesses that presently dog our society will not come from scientific discoveries. On the contrary, ridding society of sickness will come about when we look not merely at the effect, or symptoms, but the causes of the disease. And that cause stems from our conditioning—our individual conditioning, as we discussed earlier in the case of Janet, and societal conditioning.

Break that cycle of pain. You can, if you will. Instead of focusing in on negativity, keep you focus on the positive, the uplifting. Rather than watch all the gore and mayhem on the television screen, ingest words of comfort, images of beauty and true love. Do not fill your belly, your mind, or your emotions with junk food. Love yourself, and give to yourself the gifts of nourishing food, enlightening thoughts, delightful emotions.

Too hard? No, it really isn't. But you are the one who must make the choice.

Are you tired of living in a hell? Of being ensnared by the negativity and fears rampant in today's world?

If you are, you will find the strength. No matter how weary you might be, once you make the commitment of turning your life around, you will find a sense of quiet encouragement prodding you on.

That does not mean all the negative conditions in life will go away immediately. However, in reacting to the negativity around you, respond not in kind but with a different approach. Reply with positive thoughts, with unconditional love and with your level of understanding.

If you watch the news and see a family's life shattered by a fire that has destroyed their home and robbed them of all their possessions, send those people your prayers. Pray for their recovery, for their comfort, and their well-being. In your mind's eye, see these people recovering all that was taken from them. Pray that their tragic experience can be turned to good use by making them more aware, ready to create a new and better future.

So too in war-like conditions. When we watch the news and see the needless slaughter of innocents caught in a dispute over a boundary line, do not throw your hands up in dismay and question whether mankind can avert a global holocaust through nuclear war. Do that and you too are feeding the negative situation.

Recognize that the leaders of a country truly do reflect the consciousness of the people. Realize that the collective is indeed caught up in the morass of material accumulation. Be aware that dark forces have these leaders, and consequently these people, in their grip. And then work to resolve the conflicts.

How? By the power of your mind, the power of your creative visualization. See the country in dispute as being healed, made whole, and resolving the differences that have flared into war-like conflicts. Visualize the people of this country as gaining knowledge from their experience, so that they too can make a better life for themselves and their countrymen. In your prayers, in your reflections, in your moments of creative visualization, send love to the world.

The world is in dire need of it. Your prayers, your love, your creative thoughts will have an impact, and eventually will work their effect.

The more you clean up your own act, the more effect you will have upon the world. Wars reflect the inner wars within mankind in his present state. Change that state, and you change the conditions. Make peace within yourself, and you are more likely to see peace within the world.

With leaders like these, you might ask. The leaders of a nation reflect, and reflect incredibly accurately, the state of the people of that nation. All of us, as individuals, are part of the collective, part of society. As such, our responsibilities are not merely to ourselves, but to our brothers and sisters, and to our community.

You can't opt out of being involved. For you are involved. Even if you were to go off to some mountain region, find a shelter for yourself and devote your time and energy merely to your own personal evolution, something would be missing and something would be extending beyond your sheltered life. The thing that would be extending beyond your own personal life style is the ripple effect of the pebble in the pond. By changing your energy patterns, by accelerating your growth, you change the energy patterns on our earth.

Some of the greatest masters who walk the earth are unknown to man. For some of these masters do indeed cloister themselves away to do GOD's work, while they live on the earth plane. These are individuals who have transmuted the base metal of human emotions and have realized the CHRIST-like consciousness. They are individuals who may no longer need the lessons in interactions—- the relatedness with others, or the involvement in community.

For most of us, however, retreating from the world is exactly that: retreat. Progress through life is accomplished through meeting our challenges and opportunities and gleaning the lessons to be learned in each one. Two of those avenues are in our personal relationships and in our interactions with society's conditioning.

By opting out, you may be copping out.

We are here to realize the spirit in matter. As we will discuss in more detail shortly, the mystery of Golgotha with the crucifixion of JESUS THE CHRIST provided mankind with the victory of spirit over matter. The ascension of that "miracle" is a transcendence each of us is here to perform. First, by realizing the spiritual side of ourselves, and secondly, the victory of our spirit over the confines of our material world.

We cannot make that ascension if we retreat from the material world. Rather by involving ourselves in the world, in the community of man, we have the opportunity not only to raise ourselves in consciousness expansion. We have the opportunity to help our brothers and sisters along the way.

Our society is out of sync with reality. There is much to be done, much to be relearned along the way. Will you be one of us who is ready to steer society back into harmony?

If you choose to do so, choose to do so now. For that is all there is. Right now.

How? From this book, from other guideposts along the way, you have an inkling of how to turn your life around. You are beginning to realize that your own growth and development can be done by only one person—- and that person is YOU.

We have touched upon the individual's responsibility, the opportunity for self-mastery through relatedness and from choosing to go against the societal grain.

In the next section, we will talk about our earth, our environment, some of society's beliefs that we have accepted as knowledge, and have you consider alternate truth, or what may seem to be possibly disconcerting other realities.

Our Earth, Our World

Our earth reflects mankind. The conditions on our planet earth reflect the conditions of the collective consciousness of mankind.

This planet on which we live has been called the planet of the cross. For the earth is a testing planet, a space in time where humankind has the opportunity to go through a myriad of experience. In order to grow, to learn, to evolve.

The crucifixion of JESUS THE CHRIST on the cross at Golgotha was no mistake. It was a lesson, a divine teaching for each one of us.

But what have we learned from it?

Unfortunately, the majority have learned little. Instead, they wait complacently for the divine savior to return and provide them the way.

The second coming is not to be expected in a wave of glory, with the heavens opening up and gilded chariots coming down to lead us from our lessons, from our experiences. The second coming is when we, as individuals, realize the lessons of the crucifixion. For the ascension occurs with the victory of spirit over matter. This is the crux of the matter, the ultimate testing for each one of us on our planet earth.

By our individual efforts, we grow toward that victory. And in the process, by our examples, we impact the collective. Like a pebble in the pond, the rippling effects of our lessons learned.

Although we are given a home with all the conveniences imaginable, with resources in abundance: look at what we have done to our earth. We have acted like overgrown children throwing a tantrum. Instead of caring for and nurturing our planet, we continually operate from a destructive mode.

Without any regard to the consequences involved, we have raped our mother earth. We have taken from our earth, with no intention of giving back in return. We act as through the earth itself were but a tangible, inanimate object. A monopoly board on which we play our games, act out our fears and sense of lacks.

In the process, we have destroyed sections of our earth that once were abundant with plant life, with vegetation that could feed millions upon millions of our brothers and sisters who do not have enough food to eat.

We have cut down our trees, our forests, our woodlands. We, have fouled our lakes, streams and rivers. We have injected chemicals into the soil, always seeking immediate return for our efforts. Never seeking to give back, except the minimum outlay.

The North American Indians, when confronted by the encroaching settlement of the White Man, never understood the concept of ownership of land. It was a term foreign to their realities. Consequently, the White Man "bought" the land by treaty negotiations, or took the land by conquest. For ownership, possession, was a necessity for the White Man's world.

The Indian, on the other hand, understood true reality: MAN IS HERE TO CARE FOR THE LAND, NOT POSSESS IT.

Quite some difference, with radically different results. A land of plenty that the Indians had served as guardians for, became a land of optimum use.

Man came, he saw, and he conquered. In doing so, he sowed seeds which we in our present day and age are now reaping. And the harvest?

Under agribusiness techniques, food production has peeked and the land despoiled. The amount of soil erosion in the world is phenomenal. The topsoil that remains has been sterilized by chemical additives in the form of fertilizers and pesticides.

The poisons aimed at increasing the abundance of our land has, in turn, turned against us. Chemicals are seeping into our fresh water supplies, into the underground aquifers that give us our drinking water, our potable water supplies.

Only now, years later, are we becoming aware of the effects of our misuse of knowledge, our misapplication of technology.

The lush forests and wilderness that once were part of our planet earth are no more. Either by stripping away the mountainsides in exploration of minerals, or the clearing of tropical forests to create fragile savannahs on which livestock can graze and roam. Even in the furthest reaches of our earth, man has left his mark. Industrial activity and of our choice in energy sources, we have polluted the atmosphere to such a point that primeval forests, distant preserves far from modern man's direct intrusion, have been affected. Acid rain, our effect upon the atmosphere, creates precipitation so acidic that wilderness lakes have become lifeless, incapable of sustaining life in their once crystal pure waters.

Our earth is going through an accelerating process of desertification. Where we, humankind, have turned lush areas of our plant into deserts. *Turning abundance into lack.*

But why? Why should we be creating lack from abundance? It all gets back to our selves— the sense of lack each of us feels, the negative emotions we broadcast into our environment, the state of humankind's collective consciousness.

The negativity of our consciousness is destroying our planet, and in the process, our selves.

It does not have to be that way, no matter what some of the doomsayers might say. The doomsayers have their audience, because they are broadcasting fear, an emotion so conditioned within us that it is like a button easily pushed. What the doomsayers forget, however, is the potential for change.

There is always the potential for change, a change in our consciousness and consequently, the change in our conditions.

Never forget that. If you do, you are creating a set of limitations that will be very hard to break through. There is a saying—a false one—that the more things change, the more they remain the same.

We have been taught a lot of falsities. As we have discussed before, our education system is not to educate our selves, but rather to condition us to a set of accepted beliefs and attitudes. With potentially dire effects, unless we question society's ways.

But question them we must. For we must re-educate ourselves to the true reality. Not merely the appearance of reality, but the substance behind the image.

We have talked about some of the points for re-education regarding our individual purpose in life, the opportunities in relatedness, the power of group dynamics. And now we will talk about more of them.

One is a belief regarding the earth itself. THE EARTH IS A LIVING ENTITY. The earth is not a monopoly board on which we can act according to our whims, with no consequences from our actions.

Man once believed the earth to be flat. The earth is not flat. But neither is it round. At the turn of the twentieth century, man became increasingly aware that the earth's surface had changed through times past. Known initially as continental drift, now known as plate tectonics, earth sciences recognize the earth's surface to be a mosaic of plates, which like floating rafts move across the face of the earth, sometimes sliding past one another, sometimes crashing into one another, sometimes one overriding another plate.

This scientific discovery advanced our recognition of our planet as the living earth.

Yet, it is a scientific discovery we have not fully integrated into our living. We still believe that we can do to the earth what we will, and without any consequences from our actions.

Have you ever listened to the earth? Have you ever stopped a moment to reflect upon our planet and wonder about the cycles our earth mother is going through?

If you would, you would hear a cry of anguish, for our earth is close to the brink of dying. Thanks to man's unconscious actions.

All the negativity we have heaped upon our planet has

affected our earth. Despite the increasing evidence all around us, too few of us really see what we are doing to our earth mother. Too few of us really care.

Part of the problem is our sense of limitation. We see the earth as some huge body, far beyond our individual impact. But it is not.

Do you remember some of those wonderful myths and legends from when you were a child? One that always fascinated me was the story of Johnny Appleseed and the image of a man, one man, walking across the continent dropping seeds along the way. Perhaps only a myth, maybe only a legend, but in that story is the seed of truth.

You and I influence the conditions on our Earth

Don't believe the earth is too great, your vision too small, to work wonders on our planet. If you do, it creates a feeling of disconnectedness. And there is already too much of that.

We are connected. Connected to one another, to the other species that make their home upon our planet, to the cycles of our earth itself. And the earth is not some isolated planet in the midst of a vacuous void in a lifeless solar system. The earth is connected to the other parts that make up the whole. Our temperature, our seasons, our cycles in agricultural production are all related to our earth's positioning in the solar system, in relationship to the sun, and the other components of this system.

The days in which we live are a phase in our earth's cycle when we are likely to see increased earthquake and volcanic activity, changing climate conditions and bizarre weather systems, natural catastrophes that are likely to shake us to the core.

If you wish to see the earth's spasms as punishment, that's your choice. However, you could also take a different view. You could recognize that similar to ourselves, with the cleansings and purifications we must go through as we evolve in our own lives, the earth too has a process of purification.

It has happened before. Countless times, the earth has gone through a cleansing period, a transition period during which significant changes take place among the species inhabiting the planet earth. Some are recorded as the flood legends that every religion and culture tells about in their traditions. Others are noted with the shifts concurrent with the phasing out of the dinosaurs, and with the mutations and adaptations that life on the planet goes through.

At times, the earth's changes are gradual. Other times, they are quite dramatic. Sometimes, they are the result solely of the earth's natural cycles. And then there are times when the earth's changes are aggravated by man's influences, man's actions.

Many of the forthcoming earth changes are in truth the consequence of mankind's own actions, our misuse of knowledge and the wrong application of our technology. Our own actions vis-a-vis our earth are the result of an incorrect perspective.

Few people would accept the concept our earth as a dynamic, living-breathing entity. The might accept the idea of a living earth, a planet on whose surface life abounds. But to think of "terra firma" as having a life of its own, that would stretch their imagination.

STRETCH YOUR IMAGINATION—Do not be locked into the accepted wisdom that may be accepted but may not be wise. It is part of the process of relearning, of rethinking, of becoming truly aware.

The Earth Is Alive

Because we have incorrectly accepted our earth to be "terra firma" and, consequently, have thrust our whims and actions into her dynamics, our earth is sick. We have not nurtured the earth. We have asked our earth to nourish us, but we have not given anything back.

You and I can do so. By planting a seed, by tending a garden. Be refusing to despoil our environment with our wastes, our garbage. By seeing the earth as alive.

One of the glories from our technological advances has been the photographs of our earth taken from our satellites launched deep into space. With the water surface a deep blue, our earth is seen as a magnificent orb, circling through time and the infinity of space.

By our thoughts of our beautiful planet earth, we can seek to make her whole. By our prayers, in our reflections, with our thanks for all that we have been given, we can send healing thoughts to the planet we make our home.

There is a belief, a belief prevalent in society today, that we should get while the getting is good. With no regard to the future or to the consequences of our actions, this attitude presumes we are here for only a short time. TIME....

What is time? Time is a measurement. Some times measure seasons, the seasonal variations of spring—summer—fall—winter. Other times measure days by the rise of the sun, the setting of the sun, and the dawn of a new day. Our clocks measure time. There are sixty seconds to a minute, sixty minutes to an hour, twenty-four hours to a day, and 365¼ days to the year.

TIME is also a subjective interpretation. Think about it. Have you ever had the experience where time seems slower than usual? Or when time flies by without your knowing where it has gone? Five minutes may drag by so slowly it seems like an hour. Other times, five minutes may pass in the twinkling of a moment. Not very objective, this concept of time.

One of the most curious aspects about this concept of measurement is its use in our own lives. We have had one example with the five minute time interval. Perhaps trivial with no real consequence, but there is another aspect of time that is truly limiting. That time is the idea of a lifetime.

Lifetime? The measurement of time between birth and death. So what's the big deal, you might ask.

Only that the interval of measurement for a lifetime is limited by the aspect of measurement itself. Can we measure eternity or infinity? No matter how many mental abstractions we might come up with, no matter the mathematical equations we might derive, there is no true measure of eternity or infinity. Only the measurement of pieces of eternity, of parts of infinity.

So too with our measurement of life and death. Although we like to consider mankind as having evolved in understandings to a point of real knowledge, we still make measurements in our own lives. A measurement that is defined from the moment of birth into the physical body of the baby to the point of death for that same physical body. Birth—death.

If we assume that earlier man was less sophisticated than our selves (a theory prevalent in our society at present), then we must wonder whether in his consciousness, our predecessors stood at the dusk of day and saw in the setting of the sun an end to life. For from the light of day, man was thrust into darkness at the turn of night. Was that the end? Had man in that one day experienced all of life, to be extinguished with the coming of night? Perhaps, we imagine our predecessors huddling in fear, waiting through the darkness of night, to be devoured or taken by death.

What a surprise, we must think, awaited earlier man when the sun arose the following day, and he was still alive. After a while, with the sun's dawning and setting day after day, man must have come to a realization that there was no termination to existence concurrent with the sun's setting, plunging earth life into darkness.

So it is with our selves. Despite our great advances in material knowledge and our discoveries about our physical world, we are similar to our imagine predecessors. For until recently, we have assumed that this measurement of a lifetime has taken into account the entire life of our being, from the point of our physical birth to the point of termination at physical death.

Perhaps we have even scoffed at what we consider to be the superstitious beliefs of our ancestors, who would bury their dead with their various tools and weapons for their journey into an "afterlife."

With our own sophistication, we have ridiculed a belief that man continues on beyond the death of his physical body. And perhaps some of us still do.

However, in recent years we have become increasingly aware that physical death does not mean the termination of our being. Rather, it is a transmutation of our essential being from one form into another.

Physical birth is not the be-all. Nor is physical death the end-all.

This belief has been commonly called "reincarnation." Various religions from all different cultures talk about such a theory, the theory that man continues on beyond death and comes back to life in physical form at a later "time."

I personally believe in reincarnation. In my own research regarding survival, I have found this theory to be true. By means of hypnotic regression, I have experienced snatches from my past lives. I have been a rich man. I have been a poor man. A beggar man, a thief. I have been a male, and I have been female. I have been heterosexual and homosexual. I have been black, red, yellow, brown and white.

Each of these different experiences has added to my evolution, to my soul's progression. As I experience these many different personalities, these varied environments, I have learned about myself. I have made amends for past actions that were inappropriate, and I have been given opportunities as a result of my past accomplishments. I am personally working through past karma.

KARMA—The law of cause and effect. What goes around, comes around. As ye sow, so too shall ye reap. As you do unto others, so it will be done to you. For every action, there is a re-action. This is karma.

Karma is in reality the experiences we are going through at this moment in time. In our daily associations with our selves, in relationship with others — friends, loved ones, society. How we react to certain situations, how we resolve conflicts. Our karma and the way in which we work through it largely determines our dynamic interactions with our surroundings. Eventually coming to the conclusion that LIFE is our greatest teacher.

By means of my experiences through hypnotic regressions, I came to the belief that there is no pain, no horror associated with dying. It seems like falling off into a gentle sleep and awakening into a much clearer atmosphere. The realization of dying is only for a few moments. There is an experience of being lifted from the physical body, of entering into a tunnel and meeting your deceased loved ones. There is a slight confusion as to where you are. But that confusion lifts.

Having knowledge about life after death is very helpful. It will assist you in your next transition, when you are ready to leave your present physical body behind and continue your journey into the worlds beyond.

In describing the transition, let me draw upon the analogy of school. The transition is similar to graduation day, when school is over and it is time for summer vacation. As vacation begins, we talk with our school mates. We share our collective experiences of what transpired in class (our lifetime)—- what we have learned, what we did not learn; the good times we enjoyed, the hard times we endured. We reflect back on the problems we encountered that created confusion in our growth, in our personal development. Things always seem clearer in retrospect, when we are more detached and

106

not as involved in the momentary experience. We can see those we might have hurt during the school year, those we might have rejected, used or abused. As we look back, we also become more aware of our right actions and those that were not quite so right.

When we are ready to come back into physical life, we decide for ourselves what lessons we need to learn, to master, in order to progress in our soul's journey.

Let us assume that in my last transition phase, my last summer vacation, I came to an understanding that I had rejected someone from whom I could have learned a great deal. In reflection, I could see I had caused that person great emotional pain. I felt a strong empathy and compassion for that person I rejected. From this new understanding, I told my collective classmates that I wanted to go back into the next grade (my next life) to learn what it is like to be rejected. And so, I chose to come back for the experience.

I then made a decision of what school would provide me the greatest experience of learning rejection. I realized that my next mother and father (my earth parents) would provide me with that kind of experience. They are my next classroom in which to learn. So I CHOSE my mother and father, knowing full well their race, color, creed and social position. I chose them for the relationship that would provide me with the early programmed experience I would need for the REJECTION lesson. I knew of their marital relationship, how I would be affected by it at a later date.

Before I embark on my new adventure, the next classroom in earthly life, I am shown the whole scenario of my future life. I go to what are known as the Akashic Records, where everything that was, is, and shall be, is recorded (Your super consciousness).

I see the day I will be born, the day I will die. I see everything in between. I see my early relationship with my parents, the early rejection experience. I see the day I will be born, the day I will die. I see everything in between. I see my early relationship with my parents, the early rejection experience. I see my life in school, and the rejection experience. I see my enlistment in the naval service, and the rejection experience of my ego. I see my marriage, and the rejection in personal relations, and I see my divorce. I see the progression of rejection experiences.

However, I also know that the moment I have grown sufficiently, the moment I have truly learned this experience of rejection, I will no longer need those kinds of experiences. I will have gained a wisdom that will lift me from that programmed way of life.

LIFE IS AN ENDLESS SERIES OF EVENTS, EXPERIENCES AND LESSONS. HOW WE SOLVE THEM IS THE GIFT. Give thanks for the adversaries in your life, and they will indeed turn out to be miraculous gifts.

Knowing my future scenario before my present incarnation, I was somewhat prepared for my new adventure. Knowing full well that life is a continuous cycle of classroom—vacation, I was ready to embark for the transition from spirit into the physical.

The classroom is to learn, the vacation is to assimilate what we have learned.

Vacation was over for me. I left the spirit world and entered the womb of my mother. Remember I had chosen my mother, who by now was three months into her pregnancy. I became acclimated to the tiny quarters in the fetal position, floating around in symbiotic fluid.

And yet, although my physical body is in the process of taking form within my mother, my consciousness is very much alive. I hear both the inner and outer dialogues of my mother. I hear such things as: "Maybe we can't afford this child," "maybe I don't want this child."

All these fears, all these beliefs are transferred into the consciousness of the spirit personality in the womb, the child to be. As I lay there, I take on the conditions of my environment, and I absorb. Six months later, after nine months of my mother's pregnancy, it is time for my re-birth into this physical world of great learning. As I leave my mother's womb, I am guided out into the material world by the doctor who assists in my physical birth. He slaps me across my backside. I yell in protest, the primal scream of my self-assertion.

As I cry out upon entering the physical world, the doorway to my remembering consciousness closes tight, my memory of all past lives, of all past experiences, vanishes from my consciousness.

I have no recall of my past, nor do I remember what I have asked to learn in this lifetime.

I am now in the cold, cruel, physical world, starting as if from scratch. At this moment in time, I am very psychic and loving, and physically very dependent. I cling to my mother as my security blanket. My training starts. The programming, the conditioning of my lifetime experiences begins to manifest. I have entered the classroom for another round of learning, of lessons to be mastered.

And so it goes. From physical birth to physical death beyond, through the transition into the spirit world. Then back. There is no end, no finality, no termination to life. Physical death is but a transition, a transformation of the soul from its physical bondage into its spiritual life.

Can you believe that? Can you honestly believe in the truth of reincarnation?

Nothing is ever as true for us as that which we have experienced. And the fact of the matter is that many of us have likely experienced evidence of life's continuity, indications that physical death is not the end to life's journey.

How? you might ask. By witnessing the process of a loved one's transition. Not the sudden wrenching from life by violent death or sudden death. Rather, the slower process of dying.

If you have ever shared in another's experience of making that transition, then you are likely to be aware that much of his dream state, even waking state, is focused on people he has known who have made the transition before him. His thoughts, his dreams often incorporate deceased relatives or friends.

Although some may say that these dying people are going through delusional states, in reality they are not. For just as there are guides along our way, so too do our loved ones come back to help us make the transition from the physical state through death into the spirit world.

Until recently, this attitude would have seemed a superstitious belief handed down from "primitive" man. However, research on terminally ill patients has confirmed this fact. And those touched by a near-death experience corroborate this understanding.

If it is difficult for you to accept this fact,that is OK. As I said before, the greatest teacher is our own experience.

For myself, I know the truth of what I say. I know it because I have experienced the near-death experience. And it is an experience I would like to share with you.

It happened many years ago. I was having dinner with some friends. It was an elegant affair, candlelight, wine, good food and wonderful company. However, as I took my first bite of food, my mouth and throat began to feel strange. My nose started to run.

Minutes went by, and my throat became very restricted. I found it difficult to breath. Then my nostrils began to close as well. I could hardly breath.

Suddenly, I was filled with panic. Leaving the dinner table, I headed for the bathroom. My body was heating up. Perspiration dripped from my body. I felt delirious, and wanted to vomit.

I had to literally fight in order to breath. Yet, the more I fought to breath, the more restricted my throat and nostrils became. I banged my fists against the wall.

By this time, my friends were aware of my predicament. They raced into the bathroom. I know they must have asked me a million questions. I heard them, but I could not respond.

Instead, I pointed to my nose and throat. Through primitive sign language, I tried to make them understand I could not breath. They tried to comfort me, but I did not want to be touched. I was fighting for my life.

Helping me, my friends took me to the elevator, down to a car and rushed me to the hospital. In the hospital emergency room, the last thing I remember was a nurse telling my friends: "Would you please get him off the desk, he is knocking the papers to the floor."

I blacked out. Then my vision came back, but it was quite

110

bizarre. I saw myself leaving my physical body in a crumpled heap on the floor. I could see my friends trying to pick me up, interns running to my side.

The next thing I knew, I was in a long, dark tunnel. At the end of it was a light, a very brilliant light. I was moving rapidly toward the light, and could hear a whooshing noise in my ears.

I felt strange, a weightlessness and I had the subtle realization that I could breath again. My conscious mind's focus was on the light just ahead of me. The light was shimmering, and very intense. As I got closer to it, it became like a misty film. I went through the light, experiencing it as a momentary tingling sensation.

And then the light gave way to the most incredible view. The only way to describe this panoramic vista is to liken it to a beautiful summer's day in the country. There was a dazzling illumination before me, the colors unbelievable, some of them beyond the visible in our physical dimension.

I could see people walking in the distance. The horizon was filled with mountains, trees and lakes. I heard sounds of great beauty, sounds beyond description. As I stood there, it was not cold and it was not hot. It was.... PERFECT.

Suddenly, I heard a dog bark. I saw a dog racing toward me. But it was not just any dog. It was the dog I once had, a black poodle named "Pepe." I couldn't believe it. An emotional floodgate opened inside me. Tears filled my eyes, Pepe jumped into my arms, started licking my face.

As I held him, he seemed so real, more real than I had ever experiences him before. I could feel him, I could smell him. I could feel his weight and hear his breathing. And I sensed his great joy in being with me again. I cried with happiness. I had loved this animal while he was alive, and now being with him again, he seemed more real, more loving. I felt my tears being licked away by him.

When I looked up for a moment, I saw a man in his forties. He was standing in front of me, smiling. He looked familiar, but I could not place him. I looked again and recognition clicked. I was amazed.

I realized the man was my stepfather, whom I loved very much. The reason I hadn't recognized him right away was because he looked so different from the way I last saw him in his earth life. He had died at the age of seventy from terminal cancer. At the age of eight, my stepfather had contracted infantile paralysis. It left his body very deformed, necessitating the use of crutches for him to walk. Later, when he was in his sixties, cancer struck. The cancer took its toll on his physical body, which began to shrink and shrivel. He had suffered greatly with the agony and pain of the cancer. And my last vision of my stepfather had been his lying in his death bed, begging me to bring him a gun so he could shoot himself.

But now before me, he was standing straight and tall. He was not using crutches. There were no deformities. Instead, he appeared to be in a state of perfect health, looking as if he were in his early forties. I was completely overwhelmed.

Again, a surge of emotions filled me with joy. This man, in this new body, was my beloved stepfather. I placed my dog on the ground and stepped forward to embrace my stepfather.

Suddenly, I heard a strong voice was heard in my consciousness, telling me: "not yet!"

I did not understand. I screamed out: "Why?!"

Then this very strong inner voice said: "What have you learned? And whom have you helped?"

I was dumfounded. The voice seemed to be outside myself, as well as within. Everything stopped for what seemed a moment. I had to think of what was asked of me.

I could answer whom I had helped. But I could not answer what I had learned.

While this was going on, I could feel the presence of my dog moving all around me, tugging playfully at my pants. I was pondering those two questions in my mind, I kept hearing them over and over within my consciousness. As I reached to embrace my stepfather, I looked into his eyes, which were filled with the greatest love. I heard him say to me, "I love you, my son!"

At this moment I shouted out, "I love you, Pop!" He seemed

to be only about ten feet from me.

My vision moved along the horizon and there, standing hand in hand, were my dear grandparents, looking radiant and healthy. They were beautiful, youngish looking, smiling and waving to me. My heart at this time was experiencing emotional joy, a release, a freedom of knowing that we never die, only the old outer shell is discarded.

We remain the same reflection, the SOUL reflection as the physical body once was. Then I heard other barking, and there appeared a few of the other dogs I had once had.

There is really no way possible to make you believe what I tell you as truth, unless you have the same experience. As I stood there for what seemed to be an eternity, I wanted to embrace and be absorbed and merge. I wanted to stay. The unbelievable sensation of not wanting to come back is so overwhelming. That was the moment I felt myself being pulled away and back. It is like I have gained the knowledge, I have had the experience, I have expressed my emotional feelings to the ultimate. I could not prevent my returning into the tunnel of narrow focus.

It felt like a giant magnet was pulling me. My heart was going in one direction and my physical body in another.

I did not even have time to say good bye. Yet I had the most extraordinary feeling that I will see them all again. There is no time and space there! I was now racing backward in time, in the long dark tunnel, the light at the end was fading rapidly.

This time the whooshing sound was even greater. My consciousness was being stretched like a giant elastic band ready to snap. When I snapped, I awoke in a subtle state of shock and a light pain in my body. I was now back in my body, and the first thing I witnessed and experienced was the hypodermic needle being plunged into my arm.

I heard a voice say: "Welcome back." I never asked who said that nor did I care at the time. It was told to me that I was out for at least 10 minutes (dead). Brain cells begin to die in four minutes!

The cause for this incredible event (experience) was an

allergy to pine nuts used in pesto sauce which I ate that night! My experience is similar to those shared in the books of Elisabeth Kubler-Ross, and Dr. Raymond Moody and a whole series of books relating to clinical death, as experienced by many others.

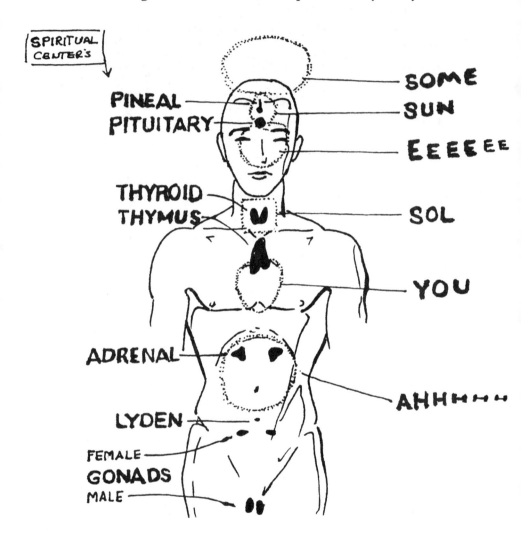

Breathing is the most important thing that a person can do for developing psychic energy and expanding inherent psychic talents. This chart is to be utilized in conjunction with the chapter beginning on page 119.

114

Past, Present, Future— An Inner Process

This technique employs a sense of finding oneself—forgiving oneself, and loving oneself. We do suggest some very soft music for the background, such as the tape cassette of *ANGEL LOVE!* Keep the music soft, so as not to distract your focus.

Find the time each day, when you will not be disturbed any any outside intrusions, such as family, loved ones or friends. Let them know that you want this time to be alone and meditate. That's all you tell them! Do not share the process you are about to do with them, unless you know they are very sincere. For there is a metaphysical law that states the moment you tell something (SHARE) you weaken it.

My suggestion is to perform this technique in a comfortable chair, sitting in an upright position. Do not do it lying on your back, for you might go to sleep, and lose the process. Make sure the spine is gently relaxed. Loosen all restrictive clothing which might refocus your attention while doing this technique. Place your feet firmly planted on the floor in front of you. *DO NOT* sit in a cross-legged position for this exercise!

Begin by closing your eyes, your hands face down upon your knees or thighs, and breathe with a balanced breath. A balanced breath is equal counts in to equal counts out, thru the nostrils only. If you can breathe out for the count of seven, breathe in for the count of seven. If you are short of breath you may use a five count or six count.

Remember, breathe in very slowly and out slowly, so gently and so delicately that you can hardly feel it or sense it. Then you are doing it correctly. Gentle breaths in and gentle breaths out, or even balanced breath. Find yourself becoming centered.

Heavier breathing might create a clogged nostril. Remember, gently and slowly.

After about five minutes of this BALANCED BREATHING, you will sense an altered state of consciousness, where your whole body feels relaxed. If you want to help the process, you suggest to yourself that with every breath you take, your body will become more and more relaxed. Deeper and deeper...more peaceful and calm...very relaxed. After a few of these auto suggestions, your body will respond.

When you begin to experience yourself on the borderline of complete relaxation, begin the process.

1. *VISUALIZE,* and if you cannot visualize, then *SENSE* yourself sitting on a deserted beach just before sunset. It's late spring, the day is beautiful. You hear the occasional cry of the gulls. Your gaze is out over the water and into the horizon. It seems you are deep in contemplation. There's no one on the beach but you. Suddenly you sense the presence of someone near. And from the left hand side you hear a small voice say, "Hello." You turn and see a little child. If you are a woman, let the child be a little girl. If you are a man let the child be a little boy.

2. The child is about 4 or 5 years old. Its eyes are bright with the joy of finding you. The child comes closer, stands in front of you, and with a big smile, it says "HELLO." Then with a flash of light, you discover that the child standing in front of you, is *YOU!* You see yourself as that young child, so filled with love and dreams and hopes. You observe the child, knowing full well what it has gone through, and will go through. You know the direction in life it will take, you know the pain it will experience, you know of the hurts and fears it will learn by, the mistakes, the joys.

You look at the child, so innocent, so guiltless. Your heart opens. Do you feel that you want to help and guide this child, so it doesn't experience what you have experienced? You can't, for that child is you. You can't change history, only be guided by it.

3. The child looks right into your face, directly into your eyes, with a love so powerful...its little arms reach out to you in love.

4. You reach forward to embrace the child... you hold him or her close, feeling that both of you merge one into the other. You love this little child so much, so beautiful, so free, so full of hopes and dreams. You embrace the child within...You hold on to that portion of yourself, embracing and merging until you feel enveloped by love, and sense that you and the child are one...You experience what that child will experience. Yet, you already experienced what that child has experienced, therefore you have a sense of greater compassion, a wider acceptance, and in reality you VERY MUCH love that little child.

5. Just allow all those faint felt feelings to manifest. If you feel you want to cry...do so. These are your feelings! Give yourself enough time to come back into the reality of the now.

6. The moment you are again aware that you are sitting on a deserted beach gazing out to sea, you become aware of another presence on your right side. You turn your head and see in the distance a lonely figure coming towards you. REMEMBER, if you're a man, make it a man. If you're a woman, make it a woman! The figure in the distance walks slowly in your direction, yet that person seems familiar. As the figure comes closer you can see it is very old. The person stops in front of you about ten feet away. You stare in amazement, for here in front of you stands *YOU* at a very old age. You look into your own eyes, and you see the wisdom of the ages. For now you are confronted with your future. You experience what you have mastered. You *see* and *feel* the most incredible emotional love. Now you observe the journey you have taken. You see lines of travel etched in your face. Your heart bursts with all the love that you feel for your wonderful future self.

7. You sense the collected experiences that you have mastered, and yet this OLD you, seems so unscarred, so unhurt, that you begin to feel an incredible transformation taking over your consciousness.

8. This OLD one extends arms out to you, for that wonderful loving embrace. REMEMBER: This old one is you, coming back from the future. As you embrace, you instantly forgive yourself for this self-imposed limitation you placed upon yourself, for the point of growth where you experienced them. As you pull your older self close, you feel the frailness of its body, yet you are enveloped in its love.

ALLOW YOUR FEELINGS TO EXPRESS THEMSELVES: TAKE THE TIME NEEDED.

9. Sense yourself completely merged with your older counterpart. When this is truly seated within your present form, sense the wisdom filling your mind. Now you have experienced your past, your present and your future. You have just experienced the SEED pattern for you upon this planet. This is to teach non-judgment, unconditional love, and a sense of being merged with your multi-dimensional self. Realize, you can always affect and alter your highest potential.

10. As you come back to the reality, you sense that you are alone on a deserted beach, but now you are surrounded and bathed in life. ALONE? You are never alone. For a few moments you have captured TIME, to experience potential!

After experiencing this process, you can always go in either direction from now on, to assist you in your evolutionary experience with soul progression. You will acknowledge an inner guidance for corrective changes you wish to make...and all destructive habits will vanish. You will be observing YOU for the very first time, as GOD views you constantly...in LOVE and LIGHT.

REMEMBER: The young child and the old you is still there, waiting to embrace you anytime you make this journey!

WORK with this process once a week, and within a month, your greatest potential will be realized. A technique is only a technique. But if you master the technique, then you become the technique. Don't expect miracles with the first try. Miracles will manifest automatically by the effort, discipline and the priority you have for CHANGE.

Developing Psychic Energy —Sonic Breathing

Breathing is the most important thing that you can do for developing Psychic Energy (Prana, Ki, Chi, etc.) and expanding your Psychic talents. (Greater Awareness) Most of the good breathing techniques we borrow from the Yogis. These practices have been used through the centuries and with remarkable results. The spleen, the appendix, and the heart are the three physical organs which transform the food energy taken into the system, into Psychic energy.

These organs act as "TRANSFORMERS" of energy. These days, everyone can help himself to a richer, fuller life, to more energy, success in their endeavors, and all of their dreams can come true.

Psychic energy is in the air we breathe, called "PRANA" or life force. The longer we breathe, the longer we live. Breath controls the body and its functions. It controls our emotions and our way of thinking. Deep breathing and meditation are two of the best things any man, woman or child can do. It brings self-realization, a better understanding of the oneness (YOURSELF) to the oneness of the Infinite (CREATION).

Breathing can retard age, or slow the aging process. The more you practice, the more you will notice that your negative thoughts will be dissolving, and the more you will become positive in almost everything you do. Breathing is *FREE*, you can have all you want...just learn to use it properly, and you will see outstanding results. It will give you a healthier, more creative mind.

When you deplete the emotional energy in the body, you deplete the psychic energy. (GREATER AWARENESS). That's why you see people growing old before their time. Negative, emotional and distorted thoughts deplete psychic energy. Psychic energy and spiritual energy are one and the same, one leads towards the other. The final goal is that all roads lead to the spiritual!

Through deep breathing, the oxygenation of the blood stream is improved, and every vital organ, endocrinal gland, nervous center, and body tissue receives better nourishment. To breathe correctly is to stay young longer. All you have to do is to look around, look at all the people you know. You will see amazing things, the way they walk, look and talk. Their personality, the way they dress. You can tell if they are breathing properly or not…most of the time they are not. And I'm speaking for 85% of the planet. Most people *DO NOT KNOW HOW TO BREATHE PROPERLY!*

Rule No. 1: AVOID NEGATIVE THINKING! One of the best books on Psychic Energy is by Joseph J. Weed. What we plan to do with this book is to change your breathing habits to a more controlled breathing practice. We will use *WESTERN* techniques which employ breath controlled by the mind. Techniques used by the DRUIDS, the American Indians, Egyptians; for the SONIC BREATHING technique, we thank our extraterrestrial friends. (ALIEN BEING).

First, select a quiet place to practice, at a time of day in which you will not be disturbed. In the Druid technique, the lungs are completely filled and completely emptied. They call it the BALANCED BREATH. Equal counts in to equal counts out. If you can breathe in for the count of seven, let it out for the count of seven.

But when you breathe in, you breathe in so slowly, that you can hardly feel it or hear it. Very gently, slowly and quietly, in and then out, repeating this breathing practice for at least five minutes or longer, per day. If you can spare the time, you will reap the rewards. BALANCED BREATH is indeed magical.

When you inhale, let your stomach come out, inflating it like a balloon. Just feel your lungs getting full. Remember, breathe very slowly with a regular rhythm or count. Sit comfortably in a straight back chair, with the back and spinal column straight, head erect, eyes closed. Your hands should rest palms down on your knees. (KNEES, ARE POWERFUL ENERGY CENTERS) This also keeps the psychic energy retained within your body, as it constantly recycles itself within the Physical, Mental, Vital and Emotional bodies.

Breathe through your nostrils only, mouth closed. And as you breathe, concentrate on that spot between your eyebrows, about one inch above the bridge of your nose, better known as the Third Eye. You should subtly experience a pulling sensation from that area of your forehead, and a heat build-up. Begin now with the (BALANCED BREATHING). This technique will enhance and extend your ability to FOCUS, and will also increase your memory to a greater degree. It will also assist in releasing the personal tensions and frustrations we create within ourselves!

Rule No. 2: Try and do all breathing techniques on an empty stomach, and for that matter all techniques should be performed on an empty stomach, to achieve greater results. Remember body and mind go together. It is further suggested by a few of the American Indians that you have a bowel movement before you perform any of these techniques. I find that to be of great value for very obvious reasons. For when the physical body is empty, the mind is more alert and aware, intensifying a greater creativity which is expressed in our everyday lives. These techniques are of great value. They have been personally selected to bring you the reader the most positive results in quickening and stimulating your own personal growth.

Next, the very powerful and yet very simple *RELAXING BREATH*. This technique was done in the Temples at Luxor, Abu Simbel, Cairo, and Gizeh, by the early Egyptians, as well as the Druids in England. Most of the American Indian nations expressed this technique among the shamans of the different tribes. It will have the effect upon you, the reader.

Take a deep full breath through both nostrils, inhaling for the count of eight (POWER NUMBER). Hold your breath for the count of six (BALANCING), and then exhale for the count of eight. (POWER NUMBER) power in receiving and power in giving. The six acts as a bridge and a balancer for both the incoming and outgoing powers. When you inhale and exhale, you breathe in with slow deliberate counts. Follow the above directions, and you will feel yourself becoming very, very relaxed, and a sense of great power manifesting throughout your body. Enjoy it!

Feel how calm it makes you feel, with a new sense of awareness that you are on the threshold of new discoveries about yourself. Never force or speed through these exercises. Savor them. Your conscious thinking can be focused upon the light (GOD) or your inner quest upon the path. KEEP the FOCUS on the spiritual!

All the techniques that we have personally selected in this book should be done sitting in a straight back chair or on a stool. Hands face down upon the knees, head erect, eyes closed. And if you are wearing any restrictive clothing, loosen it, so you will not be disturbed within the process of the technique. Remember, a technique is only a technique. If you put in the time, you will benefit *GREATLY!* The rewards will be outstanding. Once you have mastered the technique, you BECOME the technique. How much time can you give to your own personal salvation, to your own growth and well being. It's all up to you and to your personal priorities in life.

If you want to learn to play the classical piano, you have to take the lessons. If you do the techniques as a painful hardship or a discipline experience, be aware! When you do the technique because you love it, and sense the joy in renewed health and well being, then you stand to gain the greatest amount of results from it. How you FOCUS your consciousness, tells exactly where you place yourself in your everybody world of affairs, and how you present yourself to others.

Within this book I have presented my story of my own personal encounter with an alien being. So wonderful was the experience, after the initial shock left, that I am left communicating with a very unusual-looking entity from another dimension or another world. I personally feel that they are right here among us, from other coexisting realities, or dimensions of time-space. The reason we can't get ahold of them, is because they vibrate to a different frequency, yet they have the incredible abilities of materialization, in and out of our three dimensional world.

The gifts of that encounter are manifold, the experience was truly awesome in scope, as it led me to a deeper and greater concept of GOD. I can only share my experience, of how it affected me and my own personal life. Earlier in this book, I stated that I came from a background of skepticism, like I assume a great majority of the population. Yet I always entertained the sense and feeling that there was a greater world beyond, not just this physical planet.

So what I am saying, is that I had an advanced perception of something else, on the other side of our spiritual mountain. I was going to find it. Again, since early childhood I was on the quest for the GRAIL within me. There are thousands of individuals who will read this book, and experience the same things that I have experienced. Yet, each one of us is on a time frame of evolution, and if we feel the urgency, and that becomes our priority, the exploration of our spiritual consciousness manifests, and we seek the answers to the unexplained, searching for our own inner truths.

The story of that encounter is within these pages, so all I need relate is to the actual practice of this SONIC BREATHING technique. You will notice on the chart showing the chakras or the electrical energy centers, so we only work with six. Those of you who have made it a practice to meditate, balance and focus on the energy centers, will notice the absence of the seventh, or what we call the first, which would be located in the sexual region of our anatomy. It was stated by this being of a phenomenal intelligence, that if we started with the first chakra, we might get hung up in that energy center. And that these sonic sounds can and will reactivate the glands within the body of man. Medical science might be missing the boat, because their exploration does not go far enough into the other bodies that man lives within. We are talking about the Astral, Etheric, Vital, Psychic, Spiritual, Mental bodies that all men co-exist with presently. Man is more than his body. He is a multi-dimensional being. Man is in touch with the universe within as well as without. Every gland in man's body has a responsibility for all the other bodies man finds himself enveloped in. This is becoming common knowledge to millions of individuals.

To me as an investigator and researcher, and a practitioner as well, I find these sonic breathings to be the best that I have encountered in all my travels, classes, studies, and practices. I was told that the vibrations these sounds set up within the body affect certain psychic centers. You start in Beta, mid-way reach Alpha, to find your self in Theta, a very deep relaxed state of consciousness. You will find that peaceful state to be EUPHORIC!

The first sound will be AHHhhhhhhhhh. What you do with this sound as you will do with all the rest, is to take a deep breath in, and breathe out with sound. After a little practice, you will regulate your voice to come to a comfortable pitch, and you stretch that sound out as far as you can on one breath only. This sonic sound affects the solar plexus, about two inches below your rib cage. This whole area, could be considered to be your second brain. Everything, whether it be mental telepathy, clairvoyance, or healing, is manifested first within the solar plexus. It is received and sent from this region. Listen to your GUT reaction (SOLAR PLEXUS).

Remember, when you do these sounds, extend the sound as long as you can. Find your own personal level, and sense and feel the vibrations in your solar plexus area. You should also experience a heat build-up as well as a vibration in your solar plexus. You might want to call this exercise SPIRITUAL AEROBICS for your glandular system. The reverberation this sonic gives off, also helps to remove any clinging mucus to the glandular system.

1. (SOUND) AHHHHhhhhh

You're sitting in a straight back chair, feet flat upon the floor, eyes closed, head erect. Hands face down upon your knees. Take a deep full breath...make the sound (AHHhhhhhh) till the lungs are completely empty. Pause very briefly (Few seconds). Take another deep full breath and repeat the exercise. Each sonic is done three times. Pause in-between for about 15 seconds, experiencing yourself go deeper and deeper into that wonderful altered state of consciousness. Again you will notice a body heat up, due to the fact that you are exercising your glands sonically for the very first time.

2. (SOUND) Youuuuuuuuuu

This time feel the reverberation within the heart. Physical as well as spiritual. Not only does this sonic strengthen the heart on the physical level, but it opens the spiritual heart to envelop the universe. The spiritual heart (GOD CENTER) is in the right side of your physical heart. Not only is this sonic good for you mentally and physically, but very good for the voice as well! Now take a deep full breath...(SOUND) YOUuuuuuuuuu, extending the sound until the lungs are empty. Feel the vibration in your spiritual heart. Repeat this sound two more times, experiencing yourself going deeper and deeper, becoming more and more relaxed, and this is so! Pause 15 seconds.

3. (SOUND) SOLL111111111 (SOL)

This next sonic sound is for expanding your creative center, and also directed towards strengthening your thyroid and thymus glands. You should experience a subtle vibration warming this area of your throat. Now take a full breath...SOLLLLLLLLLL...till the lungs are completely empty, then repeat again twice more. Pause 15 seconds before starting the next series. Sense and feel an expansion in your neck region.

4. (SOUND) EEEEEEeeeeeeeeee

This is the special sonic that rejuvenates the psychic glands which are the size of pin heads at the base of your cheek bones. The vibrations from this sonic will affect your senses, your hearing, sight, smelling, tasting. Experience the tingling effect it has upon these areas, and in the weeks ahead, you will be amazed how the perception of your personal reality has changed. Many of the inner psychic talents will begin to manifest themselves. Now take a deep full breath...EEEEEEeeeeeeee...till your lungs are empty, then repeat it again twice.

5. (SOUND) SUNnnnnnnnnnnnn.

Concentrate all your attention to that space between your eyebrows, home of the Pineal and Pituitary glands. These vibrations are directed to your Third Eye. These spiritual centers

(CHAKRAS) need exercise also, much like your body. To perform this sonic sound (BREATH) place your tongue behind the top front teeth with slight pressure. This technique will intensify your creative talents, for greater awareness, and you will begin to experience your knowing, and an inner joy that will manifest itself as you begin to feel the EARTH CHANGES manifesting themselves upon the planet.

Now take a deep full breath...SUNNNNnnnnnnnn...Mental and physical concentration on the sound coming out of your mouths. When you have exhaled (PAUSE)...repeat this sonic exercise twice more. Remember, stretch out that sonic sound as far as possible, and repeat this sonic breath twice more. Then pause for 15 seconds, sensing every sensation you have already built up.

6. (SOUND) SOME SOMMMMmmmmmmmmmm

This last sound will be SOME. This is done with the lips and mouth closed, so a humming effect is set up. You should be able to experience the vibration in your brain, as if your brain were subtly boiling. Keep your eyes closed throughout these exercises ...and try to FOCUS your attention to that area between your eyebrows. In other words, LOOK WITHIN. This final breath is the one that seals you in a vortex of the GOD energy. These sonic breathings are in actuality KEYS for unlocking dimensional doorways to other parallel realms of time/space. You now possess the key. There is nothing to fear. This technique takes you to the highest within yourself, which attracts the outer. Now take a deep full breath...SOMMMMmmmmmmmm until the lungs are completely empty, and then repeat again, twice more.

After you have completed this series of SONIC BREATHINGS, we suggest that you go into your own personal silent space for at least five or ten minutes, and experience what will manifest. Just release any expectations, completely free yourself...and ALLOW it to happen at the level of consciousness where you presently find yourself.

Set aside a certain time each day to do these exercises. And with each day try to extend the sonic sound a little more. You will find yourself becoming more relaxed, increasing your vital energy, looking younger and more healthy. This technique also assists in healing ourselves. The more you do, the better the results. BUT GIVE YOURSELF ENOUGH TIME! As the weeks and months go by, you will see and feel definite results. Never overtire yourself. Breathing, like meditation, is a life-long study, and contained within both are the secrets of the universe and all phenomena. The longer you breathe, the longer you live.

If you are interested in bettering yourself, then this technique will open those previously locked doorways, leading to your even greater potential. Breathing is a science...one to be practiced everyday, you will be GREATLY REWARDED! This is the path that leads to SELF DISCOVERY...it's exciting!

Since that time in 1972 when I experienced that encounter, I have had some remarkable things happen to me. As it was stated, the secret is in the doing, for how long is up to you. You can't get to six o'clock before I can. If your INTENT is solid and sound, and your personal *motivation* is pure...the doors to the other dimensional realms will open wide. (KINGDOMS) Communication and love will be experienced.

As one day folds into the next, as one breath blends into the next, as one thought extends itself into the next, as one idea manifests into the next, as one step forward brings us into the next, as one sleep cycle repeats itself into the next, as one meal moves us into the next, as one minute dissolves, another appears.

Repeatable cycles, repeatable movements, repetitions expanded and extended to go beyond, on the constant spiral of perpetual gestation. All part of the evolutionary plan of the GRAND DESIGNER (GOD).

Within the repeatable cycles are new discoveries, new opportunities and a far greater potential. To discover that we are more than our bodies, more than our brains, we are CONSCIOUSNESS beings housed in physical cases for a very short duration of time, made to experience, to learn lessons, as each breath unfolds into another.

We live upon a planet of SELF DISCOVERIES, a planet of

slow primitive soul progression, so it seems. Yet spiritual evolution is forever...and forever is all eternity, never ending, always beginning, always unfolding with greater and greater potential. Yet every individual on this planet is separated by different time frames. A time in which to learn, a time to love, a time to work, a time to grow and to experience. These are the cycles of man's spiritual evolution. As we discover more about ourselves, we begin to GO WITHIN ourselves, unlocking the doorway to *true* knowledge.

Our awareness explodes with excitement as self-discovery leads us home. Within all of us are the secrets of the UNIVERSE, all knowledge of all things, of all time. What a glorious discovery that we are indeed in the image of the grand designer, the manifester of everything (GOD). What a great joy to find out that everything we have always wanted has always been ours. What sublime bliss to know we are indeed our *father's* children, and GOD loves us with an unconditional passion. We are all in preparation for our journey home, victorious and successful in resolving all conflicts that have appeared along the path, to eventually merge with this incredible LOVE!

The techniques in this book will help you explore the higher altitudes of consciousness, so you may see the distant horizons clearer, to see where you have been, where you are at the moment...and your direction into the future. This provides you with clearer sight to see the obstacles which might be blocking your path, and the ability to circumvent them. We cannot force anyone into our belief system, ideas or thoughts. There will always be provided the right time for everyone to make their own personal discoveries, about themselves and the world around them. It's time now to FREE ourselves of the restricted judgments and limitations of the collective consciousness, and become individuals who are willing to explore the RISK the herd consciousness to become truly, the...GOD...I AM!

Autosuggestion: Valuable Techniques

To those in the physical five-sense world, autosuggestion is a miraculous phenomenon. You can accomplish astonishing things with it. It can help to re-make and re-build. It can correct habits, can reshape your life for the better, and in general just bring a completely new outlook to your life.

Remember all suggestion is autosuggestion. Suggestion can be environmental, verbal, or mental. Television is a huge form of suggestion, with its constant form of the same commercials, of buy this, or get that. After a while it begins to sink in, so we find ourselves going out and getting the product. What you are doing is presenting an idea to the mind, directly or indirectly, by thought, word, tone, look, or some inner or outer agent.

Autosuggestion, it can be said, is talking to your self or suggesting to yourself. Autosuggestion is simple to perform. If done right, it can help bring you your desired goals, and help make those dreams come true, that is, if they are for the good.

Anything you do, which is not for the good, will always come back to you, so please keep this in mind. This is a psychic– mental power whose tendency is to transform itself into action.

Anything man can conceive he can achieve. Therefore, all suggestion is autosuggestion. A lot of illnesses are self-inflicted, caused by our own negative thinking, by constant repetition, and by being slightly lazy with our minds. By programming ourselves, like so and so gives me a pain in the neck. Well, sooner than you think, if you say that long enough, you'll get that pain in the neck.

Change your way of thinking to the positive side, through autosuggestion. Autosuggestion will develop new confidence, so much so that you will emerge a new and striking personality. You have learned MIND CONTROL, the method to control and dominate your mind. We have billions of little brain cells in our mind, and we end up using only 7 percent of our brain power. Through autosuggestion, you can achieve your ambitions. Learn to use your own powers and develop them to the highest degree.

If you really want to become successful, in any walk of life, concentration of the mind, through the power of suggestion, must be understood, and mastered.

Many people are suffering because they have hypnotized themselves into their present, uncomfortable condition. They are victims of unfortunate autosuggestion. Through autosuggestion you can change all that. Concentration, positiveness, and consciousness are also pre-requisites. Select your mental attitudes. You can just as well cultivate the positive, constructive kind, as the negative.

Each and every time you practice autosuggestion, you will be successful in bringing on the hypnotic state, and you will be successful in accomplishing anything you wish to achieve. By working with and developing autosuggestion, you begin to understand the workings of the subconscious mind, and understanding it, you will be able to bring it under your conscious control.

This mind-dominance can be achieved by any normal person, with practice. The subconscious mind has absolute control of the functions, conditions, and sensations of the physical body.

Today, suggestive therapy holds an important place in science, and many wonderful cures are presented at its doors. It can break open your psychic awareness, for a better you. To help yourself, it is only necessary to have faith in yourself through autosuggestion. Make your affirmations with confidence.

Believe that you can accomplish what you desire. Be positive and know that you can. And you will. Rearrange your way of thinking on the positive side, with statements like: I WILL, I

CAN, I SHALL, I AM GOING TO, IT CAN BE DONE. Tell yourself that you are getting better and better everyday.

The subconscious mind has charge of the sympathetic nervous system, which is "rested" at the base of the spinal cord. It controls the involuntary muscles, organs, and functions of the body. The conscious mind has no power to act on these, but the subconscious mind has perfect control of them. It takes command of the entire body in cases of extreme danger like shock, accidents, etc.

Now, with autosuggestion, we work in the realm of the subconscious mind.

The subconscious mind is a spiritual, creative, separate entity. It can live with the body, and also act independently of the body. It never perishes. In other words, the conscious mind cannot exist without the subconscious mind.

Now let us get to the actual practice of autosuggestion, and its techniques. The realm of self hypnosis is a total and complete period of relaxation, a peace of mind so full of contentment that life's problems and worries seem to fade away. A feeling that you can achieve happiness regardless of your station or position in life. First of all, find a quiet, comfortable place such as your own bed. Or you can fold a blanket and place it upon the floor. Then find a comfortable position upon your back, arms by your sides, feet slightly apart. RELAX.

Next, place a bed lamp, or a lamp with a blue, low voltage, 7½ watt light bulb at the head of your bed, or at your head if you're upon the floor. *BLUE,* by the way, is the most soothing color to gaze at. Now, gaze directly at the bulk in such a manner that there is a slight strain on your eyes. The light should be directly overhead, and you are peering intently at it.

Let nothing interfere with the steadiness of your gaze. Concentrate fully on the little bulb. It will appear to grow larger and smaller, as though it were breathing. Now, consciously *RELAX.* Feel your legs growing heavier, feel your arms growing heavier, feel your whole body growing heavier and heavier, deeply relaxing!

All the while, you breathe very slowly, through both nostrils, and exhale through the mouth. Keep your gaze fixed upon the blue bulb. Think of nothing but the concentration upon the blue bulb. Detach all other thoughts from your mind. Gradually, you will begin to lose all sense of feelings in your body. You will feel like lead, as if you were sinking into the mattress or the floor.

It will appear as though you were entering another world. In a short while, you will not be able to move a muscle. Gradually, you will pass into the hypnotic trance. There is nothing to fear. It is a very beautiful and relaxing experience. Now, while in this relaxed state, while conscious of your relaxation, you are able to repeat to yourself, once, twice, several times if you wish, what it is you want to accomplish. Make your affirmations positive.

You will, as time passes, and you practice and become expert, develop autosuggestion to so great an extent, that you will completely control your subconscious mind, to the point where it will obey your conscious desires. This is a simple technique that will bring fantastic results. It must be practiced daily. You must also have the desire to want to change yourself for the better.

Remember, that while doing this type of practice, you will have the strong desire to fall asleep. Be conscious of this desire and try to prevent it. That is at least until you reaffirm your affirmations.

Each and every time you practice autosuggestion, you will be successful in accomplishing anything you wish to accomplish. Remember, KEEP AN OPEN MIND! Avoid being dogmatic. There is always something new for you to learn in this world of material things. Learn to help yourself through autosuggestion.

There is no danger in this technique. If you fall into a trance, all you will do is have a good refreshing sleep, and wake up more RELAXED than before.

How To Meditate

Life is a rush and hurry and strain of affairs and events. Thoughts and emotions and activities are all a part of this modern life. So now comes the need of periods of real stillness, when you lay aside activity of mind as well as body. A time for you to disassociate yourself at will from the affairs and interests and become still in all your being. You will soon discover a balance in your being that will soften the strain and make your judgment surer.

The result of Meditation will open your Psychic and Spiritual awareness and help to attune to the cosmic consciousness, both on the Astral and Etheric planes. Invisible forces will begin to work for you. If you go into this realm of Meditation with pure spiritual thoughts and a sincere desire to better yourself, so you can help to better mankind or be of service, then you will receive a great deal from your efforts, and growth will be rapid.

Practice the techniques given here or any of the above mentioned. They are all good, and will aid you in your psychic and spiritual growth.

All Meditations should be slowly and deliberately conducted, taking time to experience the steps indicated. The serious student should meditate every day. Meditation often results in a feeling of vibrancy and lightness throughout the day. Clarity of vision comes from regular practice of Meditation.

You will find that true happiness can be attained, but its eternal source is within man and not without. With regular practice you will notice a subtle doorway begin to open and those who learn to pass through that doorway enter a new world—of spiritual betterment. You must remember, and this is very important, that if you use these techniques for the *BAD* (negative), causing harm to others, it will backlash with a devastating effect.

The object of Meditation is to impress the lower consciousness with that of the higher world. There are many good books on the subject of Meditation. If you are interested, INVESTIGATE!

Now let us get to the actual technique: If you are going to Meditate at home, bathe first, followed by deep breathing. Proper breathing is very important. Unconfine the body by wearing one light garment which will eliminate one type of physical impression from the consciousness.

You should set aside a certain time of day to Meditate, as well as the place and the duration of Meditation. What are the best hours? We have found that immediately after arising in the morning is best. The second best time will be noon and sunset.

1. Posture is important. Choose a straightback chair. Sit well back in the chair, feet firmly on the floor. Keep the spine erect, not rigid, but relaxed and straight. Head up! Hands resting on the knees, palms facing upwards. This should be a completely relaxed position. If you want, you can get into the Lotus position of the Yogis. The reason for not lying down is that you might fall asleep. Keep your eyes closed.

2. Breathing is next. We find that to become very relaxed, you start with deep full breaths through the nostrils only. This we call a BALANCED BREATH. Equal counts in to equal counts out. If you can breathe in for the count of seven, let it out for the count of seven. Through your nose only. And each time you breathe in, center your concentration on the space between your eyebrows, referred to as the THIRD EYE. Take deep full breaths, filling your lungs with prana (Energy) (Life force)

3. The next step is to suggest to yourself that you are getting very, very relaxed. Start down at your feet, and slowly work upward.

Sense and feel yourself getting very relaxed. Create. My feet are relaxed, very relaxed, my legs are relaxed, very relaxed, and so on up the body. All this under your breath. When you have reached the head area, you should be ready to meditate.

The highest point of realization should always be shared—sent out as a force for good. This practice is designed to help you realize that you are not your body, but something apart from it, that you wear the body, work with and through it.

4. Next is the object of Meditation. We have our students select an object, a picture, a bit of verse, or a person. See this all in the Mind's eye. Sense and know that it's there. Stare at the object, picture a bit of verse. Then close your eyes and see only that, the object of your concentration. Detach yourself from all outside noises and surroundings. Breathe deeply but gently.

CONCENTRATE, CONCENTRATE, CONCENTRATE. See beauty in the object. Set aside a certain period of time for this. What will come to your mind will be a great experience. ENJOY!

5. This is a subtle technique for the beginner. With time and practice, the breathing techniques will be altered and your methods will change. For the more you practice the better you become. And you will find that you can Meditate almost anywhere at any time. But again, the best place is a certain room in your apartment or home which you consider a quiet place, a place that shuts out noise and busy surroundings.

This Meditation is to be practiced daily. Now, let LOVE and PEACE and VITALITY fill your body, and make itself felt from head to toe!

We Can All Be Perfect

Perfection is like looking at the picture on the face of a packet of morning glory seeds. You look inside the envelope and you see hundreds of little tiny seeds, laying there looking limp. Yet all we have to do is to plant them in fertile soil with love and light, so they are able to manifest themselves to their fullest potential...according to the GRAND DESIGNER.

Again you look at the picture on the face of the packet, there you see this beautiful, brilliant blue morning glory energized by the sun. Its fullest potential expressed, its reflected perfection realized, its intention fulfilled. Some of us find it hard to believe that when we look at the seed and then at the picture, that the seed is already perfection awaiting the moment to become self realized, extending itself toward reaching its greatest potential, bursting forth in its magical color, reflecting back to GOD its gift!

And you say, "My GOD, this little seed is going to become that magnificent morning glory. If we could witness this with time lapse photography, that would give us a better opportunity of realizing that there is a seed pattern for everything on this planet, and throughout the universe. Who creates these patterns, you ask? The Grand Designer, the planetary architects, the mind desire of GOD? All of the above and more! Much more. We may not fully understand the mechanics of this incredible process, but in time we will.

There has to be a mind desire to take the formless seed pattern to its fullest potential—to express itself as perfection. Seed patterns alter slightly as TIME, spiritual evolution unfolds itself into our futures.

The little seed pattern for us human species (HOMO SAPIENS) is a creation so magnificent, the imprint so perfect, that we all have the potential of becoming the living GOD. At least this is the imprint of our becoming, of reaching that potential and eventually being able to express it to the fullest, according to the GRAND DESIGNER. I believe there is a grand designer behind every man and woman on this planet.

This planet (EARTH), the testing planet is the classroom to express our potential to its zenith, and then go beyond. We are presented with FREE WILL and FREE CHOICE. Some individuals have no idea what that means. Yet behind the free will and free choice is the Grand Designer. At a very young age, we develop our own ideas of earthly distortions, parental programming, and taking on the conditions of our environment. The seed pattern begins to change its shape.

We are influenced by the human family, and the parameters of our original seed pattern take on grosser form. We present ourselves with limitations and doubt, so we begin to shrink our potential for whatever time frame or life time we might be trapped into at the moment. We will all eventually reach and express our seed pattern in all its superb brilliance.

Do not be saddened by these words, because the seed pattern of what you are meant to become is already with us. It's imprinted within the higher self, the reflective image of GOD manifested in all humankind. As we distort that image of GOD within ourselves, the communication between you and your higher self shrinks and fades from our conscious view. Society's view (MAINSTREAM, Homo Sapiens) is completely distorted, creating a momentary detour in the collective consciousness (LIKE ATTRACTS LIKE).

If all the hands that reach, could touch!, what a better world we would have. If all the boundary lines were dissolved there would be peace on this planet! What do I mean by the boundary lines? The racial boundary lines of color, ethnic, male-female, national (NATIONS), rich and poor, religious, political, financial, academic, property, personal boundary lines by choice. There are hundreds more, all created by the false EGO, that separates man from GOD!

When boundary lines are created, the perfection of humankind begins to dissolve, and fade into the background, giving way to a state of precocious insanity, where we really begin to think that WE are in charge. WE, meaning the individual I. Even though we seemed to be lost in the wilderness of our own personal struggles, the emotional conflicts of a distorted ego, the *higher self waits patiently* like an eagle gliding on the thermal currents of life, observing higher atmospheres, till it needs to land to nurture and for nourishment.

Then, when the higher self presents us with a momentary merger, we sense a *high* of spiritual inspiration, we seem to have more reverence for life all around us, we feel as though we can REALLY FORGIVE our enemies and we want to spread our enthusiasm to every one around us. These are the moments of great testing, when others think you're crazy. You go beyond what others think, because in reality it's none of your business. You sense a heightening of creativity, and a presence of LOVE, so strong that it will have a lasting effect upon you, acting as a guidepost to your divine perfection—on your pathway of spiritual evolution.

As we work to realize our foothold on all the emotional conflicts which are in reality, those experiences provided by the GRAND DESIGNER, so we may learn the lessons of going beyond the conflicts of where we seem to be trapped!

Living life upon this planet is a series of incredible experiences that are actually assisting us with that eventual merger with our HIGHER SELVES. It's not going to be easy. Often it is indeed very painful. We have to experience many emotional deaths which can be devastating, as it takes our EGO, like a lump of silly putty being squeezed into different shapes, which oft-times resemble our personal thought forms. Where is divine perfection? It's there waiting patiently to be discovered.

The more you surrender to the emotional deaths, the more the closer highest self moves to help you realize that you are doing the right thing. These are the moments when many individuals begin to sense the presence of GOD within. These are the victorious moments when you discover that you are indeed divine perfection, that you can really love yourself, not out of EGO, but because you are one with (GOD). These are those thrilling moments when you feel so elated, and your problems seem to have vanished, that it's good to be alive.

Many may never experience these sensations in this lifetime. Everyone of us is on the planet to gain certain experiences, certain lessons to learn. Each one of us living, breathing, magnificent souls has a different pathway to walk. The way we live places us in different time frames. Such as a time to work and experience, a time to love, a time to die, a time to create, a time to release. And what is so amazing is that out of the 8.1 billion individuals who live upon this planet, there are no two alike.

They are separate—individual GODS in the making, making their lives the best they can, gaining the gifts of eventually reaching and successfully merging with their HIGHER SELVES. You don't have to fight it, because it's going to happen to all of us...NOW or LATER!

Man is the only one who carries around the seed of his own perfection, yet it takes the women who receives his seed, to nurture it, to nourish it, and to bring it into life. What a magical moment. Just think for a moment, that everything in the universe is mated pairs trying to find each other, so they may come together to become the one. Your lightbulb would not work, unless there was an equal polarity of both the negative and positive currents of electricity.

Man is positive in polarity, and the female is negative in polarity. And when those two polarities are in balance and become one, lights go on all over the world. That's why in relationships, both man and woman is on the hunt, seeking everywhere for their soul mate, their equal polarity. The other half of their perfection. Usually out of need and impatience, we pull in the right polarity, but with distorted circuits. Meaning bad relationships. Most of us attract into our lives whatever we may be projecting—at the moment!

Man is 70% masculine and 30% feminine, woman is 70% feminine and 30% masculine. So with that in mind, I will suggest that the moment you can release the ego (MACHO IMAGE) and begin to merge and identify with that other percentage, you become in balance with the universe and your higher selves, and the merger with perfection is close at hand. You don't have to wait.

When you look into the mirror simply acknowledge and recognize who you really are. You are perfection seeking divine perfection. You are the GOD, I AM potential. We may not express it, but we are all a little homesick for heaven. When you merge with that other polarity within yourselves...heaven is on your doorstep.

You are more than who you think you are. You are more than your bodies. You temporarily borrow these body cases for a duration of time, to carry the spirit–personality in the physical five senses world, so we may gain the necessary experiences on this plane of existence. We do not own the body we happen to be living in at the moment. We can only occupy it. So therefore, if you understand that it was given to us in trust, you will not prostitute your body by addictive habits, wrong thinking, and taking it for granted.

The human body is close to divine perfection as the universe itself. The universe follows a path of complete perfection, where humankind does not. We are the highest form of two brain variety creatures, of super animals in the flesh, with the greatest potential of become GODS in the true sense of the word. We have the potential of our picturing that manifestation. There is an inner intelligence that goes beyond that.

How can you tap into your higher self, when you have been programmed that you are a sinner, that you are unworthy, that you don't deserve? All these limitations block our view. All these limitations are only illusions we have created. We must begin to develop a faith within ourselves. No longer do you empower outwardly, you empower the GOD, within. All wisdom is at home in the higher self.

How do you tap into the higher self when you are so burdened down with your personal disbeliefs. FAITH! It comes from your heart, an inner knowing and believing. Where your inner awareness seems to expand from horizon to horizon. It's a feeling of knowing, you don't know how you know...you just know. It's much the same sensation as being overshadowed by a feeling of exaltation, or being caught in a rapture.

Your personal intuition magnified by all personal experiences and millions of past lives present a much greater knowing of right from wrong. If it resonates within your heart, it's true. Dare to think for yourself, going beyond the man-made restrictions of a misguided orthodoxy. *Most religions* have done so much to instill fear into individuals, blocking their potential Most religions were created by MAN. GOD has always been GOD, and will always be GOD! Religions will always change. Religion and Politics are both cancerous malignancies upon the FREE THINKER!

Whatever happened to the spiritual brotherhood that we had come to believe the church was providing us with? Today more than any other time in recorded history, millions are dissolving their association with the old outdated orthodoxy. Yet today the INQUISITION still exists. The spiritual brotherhood has vanished, making way for the social cults. They are all trips! If you want to follow, follow the inner teacher, the inner guru, the inner master, the inner GOD. Empower yourself as being the living GOD potential.

It's time to resurrect ourselves and realize we have never done anything guilty or sinful. In the eyes of an all-loving FATHER, we are divine perfection, we have all opportunities, we have all gifts for who and where we are at the moment. When we can recognize ourselves for the first time as the GOD, I AM, the cells, molecules and atoms, will accept that command and out-picture themselves, and the physiological features of your body will begin to reorganize itself into the original seed pattern of your intended perfection.

If you're overweight (FAT) you're going to lose weight, and mold into the perfect image that you're meant to be.

That's when you merge with your *higher self*. It's much the same as slipping on a pair of rubber gloves, that conforms to every shape. The rubber glove being in perfect form, slips onto your hand and transforms your hand into its perfection. You merge with your higher self the moment you can identify who you really are in the mirror. That's why the mirror can be your truest friend. Have a love affair with yourself, not out of EGO, but an acknowledgement to your own inner and outer perfection.

If GOD truly dwells within, at least a fragment, then how can you ever see yourself as less. I know many who go to the mirror the first thing in the morning, and stand there transfixed, looking at what the cat dragged in. They search for bloodshot eyes, crows feet at the corners, exposed pore and pimples, and snaggelly teeth. They miss seeing within themselves their own divine perfection.

I will admit that looking into the mirror early in the morning can be a horror story.

Therefore you must look beyond the vision, see and acknowledge and recognize it, the more you become. The image in the mirror reflects back exactly the way you think and the way you judge yourself. Whatever you worship, you will become. Think about that the next time you go to the mirror. Change the image that you see, see yourself in the image you want to be, and if this resonates in your heart and you begin to feel it, then you will become it!

How can you feel it, how can you tell when you're doing it right? As you look into the looking glass, and say "Mirror, Mirror on the wall, who is the fairest of them all," from the film *Snow White and the Seven Dwarfs*. It may seem difficult at first, but if you use your creative imagination with skill the image will change. If you feel it from the heart, the image will change constantly!

A simple technique to use while looking into the mirror, is to make an affirmation. An affirmation is the use of a few very powerful words that will keep you in focus and centered as you go beyond your own doubting. You repeat the statement (AFFIRMATION) over and over for about seven times, with a lot of conviction and positive determination. When you look into the mirror, be convinced that you already are divine perfection.

When you pronounce the words verbally (ALOUD) that is for the physical. When you whisper the words, that's for the mental. But when you think of the words, that is for the spiritual. When you think the words and feel flushed with energy surging throughout your body, when your head begins to bristle in the back of your neck, and when you feel your skin tingle, that's when your higher self is merged with you. That's when you are doing it right!

You can call it being very fervent with ourselves, being in the rapture of the moment with GOD. That's all it is! This is what works for me. I know that everyone is different, yet we have to have a common meeting ground for inner exploration. I cannot assume that it will affect everyone in the same way. Yet from hundreds of the shared conceptions, it works with a great deal of success.

Within us all is the spark of self realization that leads to self discovery. Everything we've ever wanted to know, is within us. The moment we stop empowering the outer, for the inner, that is when all doors unlock themselves and reveal their hidden secrets. Some individuals feel like they are trapped in their bodies. Remember we don't own our bodies, they are only entrusted to us for a duration of time. The body is meant to be utilized prematurely.

The physical body is the outer reflection of the inner consciousness. Like all living things, it has to be nurtured, loved, worked so it may enjoy the living dance of evolution. It may seem that the female carries the greatest burden. The man implants the seed within the woman, but it takes the woman to fertilize it, to manifest it into form so it may express itself in full materialization, and outpicture its divine perfection.

The woman is imbued with more intuition and wisdom for her task as the living mother. Man is still the warrior in disguise, yet the moment he gets in touch with his feminine aspect, his duality, he merges with his higher self, and eventually into the androgenous state. The androgenous state is when both man and woman merge with themselves, the masculine and feminine aspects of themselves. This will be a much higher state of perfection, where both polarities of the individual are merged equally.

Don't panic, you will have plenty of time to have relationships that will present you with some wonderful conflicts awarding you a chance to experience and grow. Eventually our hot passionate lusting will dissipate itself, making way for a highly creative, tremendously talented, satisfied being, filled with unconditional love for all humankind. A person who treats others as he wants to be treated, an individual so totally focused and centered, so spiritually motivated that he will be of greater benefit to all humankind.

Sound boring? Sound tedious? It all depends upon your point of view. Aiming for perfection is only for those individuals who have the courage to want to change themselves. Who want to go beyond the man-made restrictions of our programmed society. Who dare to be different, who are so totally unsatisfied with the present conditions on our home planet, that they have released the myth, the anchors of yesterday, to risk the fear of losing everything they have to touch the light of the universe. The universe is what is awaiting all of us in future time, a time when we will sail through the heavens and be completely at home. Many feel deeply within their hearts, that this planet is not their home. There lingers deeply within the superconscious the haunting sensation that pulls us heaven-ward. An inner working that something so magnificent awaits us all.

True perfection dwells in your heart, the point of all feeling. Today more than any other epoch of time, great changes are taking place. The prophecies of old are becoming today's reality. Yesterday is dead...LET IT GO! Move forward to the NOW! This is all we have and know! Tomorrow will take care of itself when it arrives. The GRAND DESIGNER is perfect.